Love, God

Love, God

Deborah J. Simmons-Roslak
and Linda J. Orber

RESOURCE *Publications* • Eugene, Oregon

LOVE, GOD

Copyright © 2018 Deborah J. Simmons-Roslak and Linda J. Orber. All rights reserved. Except for brief quotations in critical publications or reviews, no part of this book may be reproduced in any manner without prior written permission from the publisher. Write: Permissions, Wipf and Stock Publishers, 199 W. 8th Ave., Suite 3, Eugene, OR 97401.

Resource Publications
An Imprint of Wipf and Stock Publishers
199 W. 8th Ave., Suite 3
Eugene, OR 97401

www.wipfandstock.com

PAPERBACK ISBN: 978-1-5326-1750-8
HARDCOVER ISBN: 978-1-4982-4221-9
EBOOK ISBN: 978-1-4982-4220-2

Manufactured in the U.S.A.   09/19/18

Before We Begin

Human beings are gifted with an intrinsic drive toward the divine. Whether staunchly religious or entrenched in the struggle with belief, this very human need is reflected in various philosophies and spiritual belief systems of the world across time.

There is a deep sense of longing in the hope that God hears us, answers us and holds us closely within the dance of the divine. Still we are unsure. Theologians and mystics continue to point the way in which we are able to fully participate in a divine relationship with ultimate Love. It is a path of the heart that seeks to live and love in this way.

The good news here is that the opportunity to develop our own personal relationship with God doesn't require burning bushes, or forty nights in the desert, it does however require that we clearly see how we, ourselves, block the relationship so desperately sought through acceptance of fear and self-distain in its stead.

Confused feelings of unworthiness, self-doubt and fear of divine retribution all create a smoke screen in which we attempt to hide our hearts and vulnerability from our very Source. Fortunately, we can also choose not to put our faith in misperception rather, we can take tentative steps toward trusting the truth of divine Love, which is the birthright and heritage of every one of us.

The following pages incorporate some of the words written by theologians and mystics across time, a coordinating bible quote, a reflection and an opportunity for you as a seeker to experience the love of our creator through a guided meditation.

This path of the heart may bring surprises. It can reveal your self in relationship to God. It can help you to better understand how you use fear to turn away from the Love that you seek and it can assist you in experiencing the Ultimate Love that is the very source of your being.

Happy travelling!

> "We stumble and fall constantly even when we are most enlightened. But when we are in true spiritual darkness, we do not even know that we have fallen."
>
> Thomas Merton

There are various forms of darkness: the darkness of the sky on a dreary February day, the blackness of pre-dawn hours or wandering through days of our lives without direction, or intention. Darkness in and of it self can be delightful such as when stargazing, or it can be distressful when we feel lost and confused.

While seasons and clock-time bring fluctuations of shade with them, living a life without direction or deliberate intention becomes no more than dwelling within a deep, dark enclosure without knowledge of the self imposed prison sentence we have constructed for ourselves.

There are many who live out an entire lifetime without knowledge of their self-imposed prison sentence, experiencing every thought and action through the cold darkness of a closed heart and unexplored humanity.

Fear is the root cause of darkness. Fear of the world, fear of one's own perception of self and other, fear of non-worth, and the fear of self imposed vacuum of purpose can all be contributors to a perceived darkness. But darkness is not the truth of who we are, nor is it our inherent identity even in form.

> "For nothing is hidden that will not become evident, nor anything secret that will not be known and come to light."
>
> Mark 4:22

Take a Moment to Listen:

Sweet child: denial of light will not cause light to dissolve, just as denial of your inherent holiness and wholeness cannot deny what has been created and extended in perfect Love.

The smallest question of lack or 'other' calls the Light of Love and perfection to answer. Within Love's answer lay your complete humanity, holiness and wholeness. Grasp the Hand of Love's invitation and you embrace the fullness of who you are in Truth.

Guided Meditation

Sometimes we feel lost and confused—not knowing a way out of our confusion. We forget that there is a light to guide our way and a hand to hold.

Find a safe and comfortable spot. Let yourself relax as you close your eyes and take a breath. In your mind picture a dark and dreary sky. Picture the darkened clouds above and hear the rustling of the wind. Can you feel the wind pick up a bit and the rain begin to fall? It's ok. You are safe.

Invite God to be with you. Feel His presence deep within you. It doesn't matter how much wind or rain there is. You can feel God's enormous presence with you. Sit with God for a while. Is there a direction you are seeking? Is there a road you are unsure of? Tell God what that is. Let Him know of your uncertainty. Take your time. When you are finished, sit with God for a while in quiet. Try to hear Him tell you He is with you.

As you hear these words does anything occur to you about your situation? Is there space to think about things in a different way? Even if you are still unsure, can you feel God's presence with you? Can you know a little more that He will guide you? How does that feel?

Can you watch the clouds part now and the sun peak through? Can you experience the wind slowing down? Try and remember throughout the day that God's light is here to illuminate your mind. His Hand is here for you to hold. You don't have to decide by yourself. Love is with you.

Your Thoughts/Experience:

> "You are not a human being in search of spiritual experience. You are a spiritual being immersed in a human experience."
>
> *Pierre Teilhard de Chardin*

Are we the sum of body parts moving clumsily through years of a tainted perception of a life? The success of which is deemed forthcoming or damned through the judgment of poisoned lenses? How could that be the ultimate truth of our identity? The still small voice that calls in silence would not exist at all if this were true.

Instead, we are the union of the voice, which calls in silence and the answer, which waits to be heard. Our very existence in Truth is that which cannot be seen. In Truth the sum of body parts is the cloak through which we manifest the song that our heart creates in union with the song of Heaven. The Song of Love, which resonates within you and all of the created, is the Truth of who you are.

It is within this song that peace rests on the holy ground of your being. It is within this song that Love abides, shining warmth as it radiates throughout your perception of the physical experience.

> "Instead, I tell you, be guided by the Spirit, and you will no longer yield to self-indulgence. The desires of self-indulgence are always in opposition to the Spirit, and the desires of the Spirit are in opposition to self-indulgence: they are opposites, one against the other; that is how you are prevented from doing the things that you want to. But when you are led by the Spirit, you are not under the Law."
>
> *Galatians 5:16–18*

Take a Moment to Listen:

Holy child, the never-ending song of Love begun through very creation itself has never yielded its truth to silence, nor could it. You are the Love from which you were created. No form could reflect your magnificence. No form could contain nor isolate your truth. You are the child of Love, of Truth, of Light, and are born in the very image of the same.

Heaven's light fills you as the joy of Love brings peace and safety to your understanding of who you are in Truth.

Guided Meditation

Our identity is so rooted in how we look, or where we stand in comparison to others. We spend our lives in constant judgment of ourselves. Sometimes it's exhausting.

Sit in a comfortable place and take a deep breath. Now take another. Invite God to be with you. Think about how you see yourself. Are you judgmental about your body? Do you worry about how you look, what you wear, or what others have compared to you? Think about that for a while. Try to view those judgments as something apart from yourself. Tell God about your worry and judgment.

What would it feel like to really know that none of those judgments matter to God? What if He had no judgment upon your physical appearance, or your clothes, or your financial standing?

What if God loved you simply because you are His child? What would that feel like? If you really knew that, would it help you to be more accepting of yourself and others? How would that help you? Share this with God.

Now let yourself hear Him tell you how much He loves you simply because you are His. Sit with that love and acceptance.

Your Thoughts/Experience:

> "Happiness is our natural state. Happiness is the natural state of little children, to whom the kingdom belongs until they have been polluted and contaminated by the stupidity of society and culture."
>
> *Anthony de Mello*

Little children wonder at the world. Flowers, sky, ocean and snowflakes awe them. With open hearts and hands they accept what is presented on face value. The laughter of toddlers rings with delight and glee as they endlessly explore the world running, walking, tripping along their day. The space of pre-judgment is where the child dwells. A space where smells, tastes, sounds and sights are miraculous to behold and where one complete moment follows one complete moment.

It is an unfortunate truth that the adults in charge of children are also the keepers of spiritual toxicity. Adults systematically and consistently squeeze the wonder and awe from little children in the name of norms and expectations. Norms and expectations have no need for wonder or glee.

Norms and expectations of society feed spiritual toxicity bloating its owner. In turn, the spiritually toxic spill waste upon the young, for whom living, laughing and wondering are as natural as breathing in and breathing out. When the sheer joy of living has been acceptably terminated, the child is guided down the road to adulthood filled with societal expectations so that the process can begin once again. Unless of course one brave individual once in a while just says no.

No thank you to the norms and expectations. No thank you to the spiritually toxic spills and warnings regarding refusal. No thank you honestly. I'll hold on to my joy.

> *"You were taught, with regard to your former way of life, to put off your old self, which is being corrupted by its deceitful desires; to be made now in the attitude of your minds; and to put on the new self, created to be like God in true righteousness and holiness."*
>
> Ephesians 4:22–23

Take a Moment to Listen:

Precious child: Do you know who you are? In Truth you are no less than the delight of Heaven itself, of total and complete Love from which you have been given breath and breadth. All wonder and expanse lay safely still within your heart. No fear or doubt could erase that which you are. Come walk with Me awhile.

Guided Meditation

As a young child we gaze with wonder at the natural world. Everything is an adventure. We are simply delighted by life. As we get older, it becomes harder to remember that joy and wonder. We worry too much about all of the expectations we impose upon ourselves.

Find a comfortable spot and settle in. Close your eyes and take a deep breath. Once again invite God to be with you. He loves you unconditionally and offers you joy. Was there a place outside as a child you loved to explore? Perhaps it was in a wooded area, or on a farm, a park, or even in your own backyard. Let yourself think of it now. If you didn't have such a place you can create one.

Is there a tree with all kinds of birds? Are there interesting bugs on the ground and dandelions you can make wishes with? Whatever it is that would give you joy, you can allow yourself to explore it now. Take your time. Have some fun exploring. There is so much joy God wants you to feel. You can talk to God about your experience. Allow Him to respond. Hear Him tell you that He wants you to feel more joy in your life. Then tell Him how you might be able to give yourself more of that joy. He wants you to have it. Write down your experience if you like. You can always come back to this lovely place in your mind whenever you need to do so.

Your Thoughts/Experience:

> "As long as I am this or that, or have this or that, I am not all things and I have not all things. Become pure til you neither are nor have either this or that; then you are omnipresent and, being neither this or that, are all things."
>
> Meister Eckhart

Society conspires to wipe away the paradox that exists between perception and Truth. The conspiracy tirelessly works to disengage our experience of living, from our purpose for being. In return for our agreement, society bestows accolades upon those who achieve the proper type of profession, the proper type of accumulation and the proper kind of social interaction.

The fine print to this contract is blurry however; consequences to signing on the dotted line results in a spiritual anomie of sorts. We are not sure of who we are, what we are doing, how we are living, or even why we need to perform the functions of co-conspirator. Like good soldiers however, we carry on identifying what we have and what we do as the definitive answer to who we are. We become the function of the conspiracy, losing our direction and our identity in the process.

Somewhere along this ill-fated route lie the rewards of discontentment along with a circle of endless questions that cannot be answered due to the very nature of the relationship.

> "Know that the Lord, he is God! It is he who made us, and we are his; we are his people, and the sheep of his pasture."
>
> Psalm 100:3

Take a Moment to Listen:

There is but one identity precious child, which cannot be found in actions of fear or actions to gain yet more accumulations. You are the Love from which you were born in Truth. It matters not the form of how Love manifests its being in the world, for the function of Love is to extend and embrace without regard to form.

The Truth of your identity is the Truth of Love itself. All actions from this Truth become the manifestations of the function of Love.

There is no greater or lesser among you. You are one another as you are your Self. You are the joy of the Love that first created who you are in Truth.

Guided Meditation

We are often attached to our way of accomplishing those things we consider necessary—even prayer. Our identities become tied to what we have accomplished, or accumulated. What would it be like to identify instead with openness and freedom? How would it feel to know that God is leading us?

Go to your favorite place and relax. Take a couple of deep breaths. Ask God to be with you. Think about some of the ways in which you identify yourself. What are some attachments you may have—even attachments to forms of prayer. Can you only allow prayer to be a certain way? Do you judge other's prayers?

Now what if you let yourself feel more open or unattached? What other ways could you pray? How might God be leading you in a relationship with Him that you hadn't expected or considered? Could there be limitless possibilities for a connection to God?

How would you like to deepen your relationship with God? Tell Him. Then let Him tell you about His love for you and how He may be guiding you.

Your Thoughts/Experience:

> "In the final analysis, the questions of why bad things happen to good people transmutes itself into some very different questions, no longer asking why something happened, but asking how we will respond, what we intend to do now that it happened."
>
> Pierre Teilhard de Chardin

If what is considered 'bad' happens to those who are considered 'bad', society applauds. If what is considered 'bad' happens to those who are considered 'good' society expects the back to be straightened, while the bootstraps are pulled up. In either case, victimhood is held, by the good with the bad, or the bad with the good. Someone or something becomes a 'rightful' victim, albeit without recourse, without explanation, without hope. Holding as a truth an identity of victimhood is septic, infecting all willing to believe victimhood as both identity and purpose.

In truth, bad and good people and events are constructs of a society that colludes to separate and isolate. I am myself, but you are 'the other'. We are us, but . . . and so it seems to go. Framing a personal identity around victimhood, strangles individuals and societies, the belief in which chokes the ability to see beyond labels.

> "Yet you, Lord are our Father. We are the clay, you are the potter; we are all the work of your hand. "
>
> Isaiah 64.8

Take a Moment to Listen:

Neither 'good' nor 'bad', you simply are the extension of Love in all glory. During situations and experiences of discontent or pain, know that the intent to remain focused on that birthright allows a particular clarity of vision. Clarity of vision strengthens intent and resolve while encouraging your identity as a child of Love. Choices that you make result in a consequence of that choice, even as sometimes there seems to be no choice, just a block in the road going forward.

No punishment or pain could be meted forth by a loving creator who sees and holds only a child molded of Ultimate love, peace, and joy. There could be no loving God who is also a master of punishment and prizes. Trust that all experiences in life give an opportunity for growth in the core of who you are and as Love holds you to be.

All of Heaven stands by you, in you and with you.

Guided Meditation

Unexpected situations or negative circumstances can invite us to feel victimized by life. We might even look toward negative outcomes as our answer to confusion or general malaise. We get upset and feel like life is totally out of control. How do we respond when life's situations present us with challenges?

Sit in a quiet place and take a deep breath. Ask God to be with you. When have you felt like a victim? What was that like? It's natural to feel helpless when that happens. Sometimes we may think it's a punishment from God.

What would it be like to know that negative situations are not a punishment from God? How would it feel to know that God wants to help you? What if He were helping to guide you, rather than hurt you?

Tell God how you feel. Take your time. He wants you to open your heart and mind to him. Now can you listen for His response? Can you hear Him tell you He loves you and that He wants to help

LOVE, GOD

you? How does that feel? Do you have space to see problems in a different way? How might God be guiding you?

Your Thoughts/Experience:

> "The only true liberty is in the service of that which is beyond all limits, beyond all definitions, beyond all human appreciation: that which is All, and which therefore is no limited or individual thing: The All is no-thing, for if it were to be a single thing separated from all other things, it would not be All."
>
> Thomas Merton

Capturing wind in a mason jar and labeling it 'wind' cannot make it all of wind, just as capturing 'light' in a mason jar and labeling it as such cannot make it all of light, for both wind and light cannot be both individual phenomena yet in totality as it has been taken from the totality of their respective experience. Both wind and light exist in a totality, which then expresses its identity.

While wind and light are by far poor examples for that which is All, the examples underscore several of our human needs: to isolate, to label, and to identify. That which is All cannot be contained in an isolated mason jar and labeled by any name therefore; It cannot be definitively identified as this or that, belonging to them or those alone.

Though the All (or All there is) has been given various and sundry names and attributes across time, those names and attributes are a mere series of mason jars in which human beings attempt to isolate, label, identify and claim as theirs alone. Wars have been fought and continue to be fought over the ownership of these mason jars, which we suppose contain the right name and attributes for a god that we then claim to be our own. But this would be a god by mere human design alone and not of Truth. Nevertheless, the All remains, in expansive totality touching the edges of our willing consciousness. Let us put away our mason jars, our fear and our justifications and reach to touch that, which is in Truth, total Love and acceptance.

> *"God is not a man, that he should lie, nor a son of man, that he should change his mind. Does he speak and then not act? Does he promise and not fulfill?"*
>
> *Numbers 23:19*

Take a Moment to Listen:

It matters not which name you call upon, for each name will draw comfort, healing and unity to you. Open your willingness and your heart to that which flows through each and every person equally, as It flows through all of blessed creation.

Guided Meditation

We often want God to help us, but are confused as to what it is we really want. Sometimes we think we know what we want because our plan would be better than God's.

Sit in a relaxed position and close your eyes. Take a couple of deep breaths. As always, ask God to be with you. Is there a problem that you definitely want help with? Think of it now. What have you supposed the outcome to be? Is there only one outcome or several? How do you know which is best? How do you know which would be the most beneficial to everyone involved including you? The answer is -you really can't know.

Can you begin to see that you might not know the best outcome for a situation? Can you try and allow God to deal with the situation in His way? Ask for His help.

Try now to experience how much God loves you. Sit with His love embracing you. Then try and carry that love and experience with you.

Your Thoughts/Experience:

> "... *Life is easy. Life is delightful. It's only hard on your illusions, your ambitions, your greed, your cravings...*"
>
> *Anthony de Mello*

How fearless are we? Honestly. If we were fearless, we would have no problem asking for help from heaven whenever we encounter confusing difficulties in our day-to-day life, but most of the time we probably do not. Why is that? Perhaps sometimes we may forget to ask, especially since we're so used to handling things ourselves. Although handling things ourselves doesn't always seem to work out the way we hoped it would, being independently human, we keep on trying anyway. Why else don't we ask for help from the one source that knows how to help? Here's a thought: Trust. Trusting assistance from God doesn't sound too practical especially when we need practical, independent human help now. Hmm. How well is your method for gaining lasting assistance working for you?

How practical is asking God for assistance on a regular basis? Depending upon your frame of mind, it can seem like a no brainer, while at other times, the thought of stopping in the middle of an 'incident' of whatever kind to ask a non-physical person for help feels insane. While we readily and unwittingly trust our parents, relatives, and even coworkers for methods in handling difficulties whether they worked or not, we are not so readily willing to trust heaven's guidance.

Trusting in the guidance of heaven necessitates moving away from the little will that we suppose holds our answers and support. It also necessitates being aware of our own participation in colluding with other little wills to the exclusion of heaven. When we consciously choose the Will of heaven, over and above our own capricious little will, all assistance is ours.

> 'Our fearlessness towards him consists in this, that if we ask anything in accordance with his will he hears us'.
>
> John 5:14–15

Take a Moment to Listen:

There is always a choice to be made between a small, frightened will and the Will of Heaven itself. Each choice either brings more confusion and pain, or gratitude and gentle embrace. In any given moment become aware of that which you are choosing, then choose the Will of Heaven with certainty.

Guided Meditation

Trusting God to guide us is often difficult. Sometimes we don't even ask for His help. We just believe we have to figure it all out by ourselves. It doesn't occur to us that we don't have to figure everything out alone.

Find your favorite spot and sit down. Close your eyes and breathe deeply. Once again, ask God to be with you. He is already here, but you may not be aware. What is it that you are struggling with the most right now? What do you need help understanding? Think about it for a few minutes. Tell God what it is that is bothering you. Tell Him what you need guidance with. You can take your time. There is no rush. He is infinitely patient.

He wants you to know that you are not alone. Can you listen for Him to whisper that He is always with you? Sit with Him for a while. Perhaps something new in this space will occur to you. If not right now, there will be endless possibilities for Him to guide you. Perhaps you will read something, or hear something, or get a feeling or sense of being led.

Don't feel you have to know right now. Leave space for God to help you throughout the day and week. Trust that He loves you and wants to help you. Stay in this place of love and acceptance for as long as you need to. God goes with you—always.

Your Thoughts/Experience:

> "The church will have to initiate everyone—priests, religious and laity—into this 'art of accompaniment', which teaches us to remove our sandals before the sacred ground of the other."
>
> Pope Francis

As you look upon another, whom do you see? If you look carefully you will recognize something of yourself. You will recognize the same emotions of fear, pain and distress. You will also recognize hope and joy. So forgiveness then becomes a little easier—for others are not so unlike you.

If you can look with compassion you can recall that as God loves you in your pain and fear, does He not love them in their pain also? You will remember that your brother and sister were created in the same loving kindness.

If Love is compassionate and understanding with you—can you not open the door to your heart, just a little for others? God looks upon all of His children in perfect and sacred love.

> "But when the Pharisees heard that he had silenced the Sadducees they got together sand to put him to the test, one of them put a further question, "Master, which is the greatest commandment of the Law?" Jesus said to him you must love the Lord your God with all your heart, with all your soul, and with all your mind. This is the greatest and first commandment. The second commandment resembles it: You must love your neighbor as yourself."
>
> Matthew 22:34-38

Take a Moment to Listen:

Love is all encompassing my child and leaves out no one. Love creates in love equally and for all eternally. You have looked on another and have forgotten who you both are. You often fear you walk alone, yet you are blind to the exquisite love that is your birthright as it was also given to those that walk with you.

As you love and forgive another, you will gently watch their dark shadows fall away. Here you will recognize their beauty—for it is also yours. You were both created in perfect love and eternal joy. As you see it in another my child, you will rejoice in knowing you walk with those I have lovingly embraced just as I lovingly embrace you.

Guided Meditation

When we are in emotional pain or distress it's very difficult to remember how much God loves us. It's impossible to know when we are judging others through our own pain or distress.

Though we may forget, God's love always surrounds us. We might not be able to recognize it however, when we wrap ourselves in negativity and pain we cannot hear the call of Ultimate Love.

Find your favorite quiet spot and sit down in a relaxed position. Close your eyes. Breathe deeply. Now in this quiet, calm space, invite God to be with you. Allow yourself to experience His gentle love. Listen as God speaks softly to you. Hear Him tell you how much He loves you and how precious you are to Him. His love never left you.

Allow yourself to stay in His love for as long as you need to. He is always with you, even when you are not aware or open to that love. Now perhaps you can carry that love with you and gently extend it to all those you meet everyday.

Your Thoughts/Experience:

> "Criticism of others is thus an oblique form of self condemnation. We think we make the picture hang straight on your wall by telling our neighbors that his picture is crooked."
>
> *Fulton Sheen*

How difficult it is to kneel in mud and wrestle with all of your own perceived transgressions. How difficult it is to examine your own faults, weaknesses and shortcomings. However, doing so does have positive aspects.

We learn to see our own humanness and therefore, we can begin to notice it in our neighbor. We can learn that looking at ourselves with honesty there is nothing we need to fear. As we hold the Hand of Love Itself, we can learn to look with gentleness and even laughter. Love can and will teach us to be kind to ourselves, as we become more brave. God will love us as much in our humanness as He does every other moment of our existence.

> "Why do you observe the splinter in your brother's eye and never notice the great log in your own? How can you say to your brother "Brother, let me take out that splinter I your eye" when you cannot see the great log in your own? Hypocrite! Take the log out of your eye first and then you will see clearly enough to take out the splinter in your brother's eyes."
>
> *Luke 6:41–41*

Take a Moment to Listen:

Do not fear true introspection my child. For as you look within, you can invite me to look with you. We can look together in gentleness at your perceived shortcomings. If you can accept the kindness with which I see you, you will, in turn, develop patience in accepting perceived faults in your neighbor as well.

I look at all I see in kindness and hope. Love cannot condemn. The more you look at yourself through my eyes, the more peace you will find. Do not fear what lies underneath behavior, for I go with you and I will gently remind you of how deeply you are loved.

As we travel together through your perceptions, I can help you begin to understand the cause of your actions. We can sweep away the cobwebs of fear and leave behind a frightened need you will no longer have.

It is in the kindness of understanding my child, that you will find freedom. Do not fear introspection. It is here that I hold your hand and go with you on this inward journey. It is here that you will find true freedom and blessed peace.

Guided Meditation

Looking honestly at your self is not always an easy task. Looking at others openly and honestly can be difficult as well. This becomes compounded when we believe that God is keeping score with every thought and action we have or do.

Go to your favorite comfortable spot and relax. Close your eyes and breathe deeply. Ask God, who loves you without reservation, to guide you on this inner journey. Think for a moment about someone you are having trouble with. Allow yourself to see that person and think about what bothers you about them. Gently ask God to help you see without judgment or criticism. Allow Him to assist you to see through Love's sight. Give yourself permission to accept His healing love.

Whenever you need to, you can ask God to journey with you, or you can see the 'splinter' in your own eye. God wants you to take it out, so that you can see more clearly through His mercy and love.

Your Thoughts/Experience:

> *"The most powerful form of prayer, and the one which can virtually gain all things and which is the worthiest work of all is that which flows from a free mind. The freer the mind is, the more powerful and worthy, the more useful, praise worthy and perfect the prayer and the work become. A free mind can achieve all things. But what is a free mind? A free mind is one which is untroubled and unfettered by anything, which has not bound its best part to any particular manner of being or devotion and which does not seek its own interest in anything but is always immersed in God's most precious will, having gone out of what is its own."*
>
> *Meister Eckhart*

We are attached to those things that mirror our perception of what is positive: Personal beauty, a talent that the world applauds, a pleasing address and our circle of friends are all attachments making up the fabric of who we believe ourselves to be. Even the way in which we celebrate our notion of God is an attachment. Whose place of worship is correct? Whose form of prayer most likely heard in heaven?

Here lies the challenge: we can suppose that others might have a more superior manner in which to commune with the Almighty and that the communion derived from method a or b or c is acceptable within society, or we are certain that the way in which we celebrate our notion of God is ultimately correct, having been handed down through generations. However, the free mind, we are told, is free to explore that which we may be called in a form that may be different from the methods and ways of general society or even from generations before us. The free mind does not use its 'little will' to suppose or impose. The free mind consciously steps away from the 'little will' deliberate in its intention to bathe in the very Will of God.

While we certainly have choices to make regarding ways in which to live, our relationships or how to seek God it is the 'small will' which is our own, that is doing the choosing. Attachment to our little will, along with all of the choices it decides upon, cannot by its very nature assist us in experiencing communion with Ultimate Love.

> *"Devote yourselves to prayer, being watchful and thankful."*
> *Colossians 4:2*

Take a Moment to Listen:

Come rest your heart with mine. Together we will see through Love's eyes that which needs to be seen, hear through Love's ears that which needs to be heard, and embrace through Love's own what needs to be embraced.

Guided Meditation:

God is with you right this second surrounding you with His love. Take a moment to experience His presence.

Close your eyes and take a deep breath. In your mind, see yourself surrounded by nature. Perhaps you can imagine an old, beautiful tree with knarled, fat branches twisting upward. What kinds of wild life are home to this tree?

There is a small brook that runs by your feet. You can hear the bubbling water as it bounces from the rocks and pebbles. Hear it?

Sit under the tree and relax. Breathe in the peace that you feel here. In that peace God begins to speak to you of His Love for exactly who you are. What does it feel like to hear Him? Can you accept His love for you?

In any language or form God shares his boundless love with all that is created. His love surrounds a shared smile, a quiet moment, a helping hand and a kind word. His love is intertwined with every movement that reflects Love's Will.

Breathe in deeply. Release your breath. Feel the peace and surety of God's breath within your heart. How is it that you share His love?

Your Thoughts/Experience:

> "But the ultimate reason for our hope is not to be found at all in what we want, wish for and wait for; the ultimate reason is that we are wanted and wished for and waited for. What is it that awaits us? Does anything await us at all, or are we alone? Whenever we base our hope on trust in the divine mystery, we feel deep down in our hearts: there is someone who is waiting for you, who is hoping for you, who believes in you. We are waited for as the prodigal son in the parable is waited for by his father. We are accepted and received, as a mother takes her children into her arms and comforts them. God is our last hope because we are God's first love."
>
> Jürgen Moltmann

We are a society that idealizes academia. It is generally believed that academia and academicians from any genre of study must surely hold the answers. We revere doctors and place attorneys on pedestals. We place our hope in them. Our hope for healing and our hope for justice is trusted. We trust those who will heal us and those who will deliver justice to our door. However, if our healing is not imminent, or justice becomes elusive, our hope and our trust become cynical, or we may consider justifying the outcome. Maybe we did not deserve healing or justice. Maybe we misplaced our hope and our trust.

We have placed our hope and our trust upon other human beings to be there for us with unequivocal conviction, just as we safely store our notion of God into a personal closet with that same conviction. While we must trust and hope in others in order to maintain and grow in given relationships, placing trust and hope unequivocally upon any one human being gives another an incredibly heavy burden to carry.

Just as trust is a shared intimacy, which grows in depth with time and experience, hope is a promise fulfilled as trust deepens. We are unequivocally embraced by the very Love that created us. Love waits in patience for our tired return. What more could we hope for?

> "May the God of hope fill you with all joy and peace as you trust in him, so that you may overflow with hope by the power of the Holy Spirit."
>
> Romans 15:13

Take a Moment to Listen:

Come my sweet child into waiting arms. Your return gives heaven reason to rejoice. Place your weary head upon my shoulder, for you are home, as you are here wrapped in the very space where you began.

Guided Meditation

We walk through our day-to-day lives on automatic pilot, forgetting how much we are loved and treasured by God. Forgetting that we are the beloved and as such, are embraced in every space of time that we experience.

Sit in your favorite place and close your eyes. Again, breathe deeply. Invite God to be with you. Can you feel His presence? Can you allow yourself to experience His unconditional love and endless peace? If you cannot—ask Him to help you.

Allow yourself to stay in this space of God's love and peace. Feel yourself enveloped in His endless care. Listen as He tells you that you are His beloved child. Allow yourself to experience the sweetness of this love.

Ask God to help you remember throughout the day how loved you are. When you forget, you can ask Him again to help you remember.

LOVE, GOD

Your Thoughts/Experience:

> "When we are at wit's end for an answer, then the Holy Spirit can give us an answer. But how can He give us an answer when we are still well supplied with all sorts of answers of our own?"
>
> Karl Barth

Anyone who has had experience with tired or confused children also has experienced the bedraggled way in which they communicate wants or needs while in that emotional state.

"I'm thirsty," they whine. "Here honey, would you like some water?" you answer hopefully. "Noooo, I don't want thaat," the answer comes swift and sure. Nothing you offer is acceptable, yet they are thirsty and want something, even while they're not sure what that something is. Though they seem to believe that they know. "I want Sugar Wow, I want Sugar Wow." Sound familiar? In much the same way we ask, "Lord, I really need you to help me with this situation," even as we have already envisioned a dozen scenarios in which God could help that would be acceptable to us. Should, heaven forbid, the answer is not one we wanted, then we are either angry with God or ourselves or both also for reasons we have already worked out somewhere in our psyche. Much like an over-tired, or petulant child we ask or demand help from heaven, but it had better be in one of the ways that our 'little wills' have imaged it should arrive.

Unfortunately, like children, we are not privy to all of the ramifications of an answer that we have worked out for ourselves however, God does know and knows exactly what we need. Cynical?

The next time you need assistance ask God to help with whatever you need helped, but allow God to then do what Love does best. Try not to get in the way.

> "Ask, and it will be given to you; seek, and you will find; knock, and it will be opened to you."
>
> Mark 7:7

Take a Moment to Listen:

Child of heaven, all clarity is freely given when you find yourself confused, or fearful. No holy child would be left in such a quandary in pain and alone. No ultimate love could extend such cruel neglect. Do not imagine answers in fear or discontent rather, seek the peace within you, where Heaven and Spirit await your willingness. Breathe in that holy space and know that you are loved.

Guided Meditation

We recognize the state of anxiety and of being 'at wit's end', but we often do not recognize Love's healing hand. There may be some days when feeling anxious or confused is more acceptable to us than accepting the gifts of our inheritance.

God wants to heal your heart. Whatever pain, anxiety or sadness you feel can be healed with His peace.

Find a comfortable place to relax. Close your eyes and take a deep breath. Breathe in and out deeply a few times. Focus on those breaths. See yourself by an infinite ocean. The waves rise and fold meeting the sand in rhythmic harmony. Watch the precise majesty of those waves. The salted air is pungent with spray stretching crazily toward the clouds. You are alone on this stretch of beach, but not completely. God is here with you.

Allow your heart to speak. Know that He is listening with total and complete healing peace. Allow yourself to hear His answer. Rest in that answer. Rest inside that healing peace.

Your Thoughts/Experience:

> *"Perhaps nothing helps us make the movement from our little selves to a larger world than remembering God in gratitude. Such a perspective puts God in view in all of life, not just in the moments when life seems easy."*
>
> Henri Nouwen

'Thank you' or a derivative of such is available in any form for use by human interaction. Simple enough. Someone extends himself or herself and our response is 'thank you'. Should someone extend himself or herself a bit more we add 'so much' to the end of thank you. Should the extension of kindness show itself in a grander gesture we add emotion and positive body language to our 'thank you—so much.' The displayed emotions, positive body language and 'thank you—so much really' is registered by giver and receiver in gladness. Both have given and received. Such as it is with thank you.

We are appropriately thankful upon appropriate occasion. We are at the level of appreciation. We appreciate having been appreciated, while others appreciate having been remembered. We have both given and received. We are thankful—for the moment.

While the act of exchanging thank you may resemble the state of gratitude, the pair is actually on opposite ends of a continuum. The act of saying thank you at the very beginning while the state of gratitude, deepening exponentially, as the continuum extends itself within the human experience.

Gratitude on the other end of the spectrum is where we hold our appreciation for a remembrance given, an opportunity to remember and find gratefulness when there is no remembrance at all. We are outside of our need to be remembered because we've stepped outside of our little wills and small selves. In deep gratitude, the rain clouds, or sun, small insects and screaming children can be experienced for their Reality. They are simply the pure Love of the Creator, and then, we can experience our reality also. We are simply the Beloved of Love Itself. Thank you doesn't seem quite enough.

> "And let the peace of God rule in your hearts, to that which also you are called in one body; and be you thankful."
>
> Colossians 3:15

Take a Moment to Listen:

In the fullness of All there is you were conceived. In the richness that is your inheritance you are swaddled. Reach to touch all that is yours from before even time itself began. You are the heart and joy of the Creator and the Love of existence entirely.

Guided Meditation

What would you like to tell the people in your life who love you? What would you like to say to those in your life who have guided you, prompted you or lifted you up when it was needed? Co-workers, random meetings with people whom you may never meet again might have lifted your spirit, or encouraged you when needed. Does that deserve a heartfelt thank you, or a sanctified prayer of gratitude?

Imagine living in a place where gratefulness comes easily. It floats on the very air that you breathe. In a quiet space, think about how you understand gratitude. Have there been moments in time when you have taken friends, family or co-workers for granted? Of course it didn't feel that way in the moment, but did the depth of gratitude fill you as you thanked them for their kindness? Have there been times when you might have forgotten or taken for granted the depths of God's incredible and unconditional love for you?

Breathe in deeply and exhale. Breathe in the gratitude that God holds for your very existence. Allow it fill your lungs, stomach and all of your being. Gratitude breeds sheer joy.

Breathe in the joy that God holds for your existence. Gratitude and joy fills all who are open to the Ultimate Love from which we were all created. As you breathe in that gratitude and joy, so are you able to share the same with every one around you.

Your Thoughts/Experience:

> *"The Christian of the future will be a mystic or he will not exist at all."*
>
> *Karl Rahner*

Among the must do's, the can do's, and feverish scheduling for future do's the soft call of the hungry heart restless to find the pathway homeward asks of us to hear its' need. A heart-call can make itself known in any recognizable form, but how is it possible to fill the need for the mystery that is God's every present light and love? How can we fill the need of our heart with an unfathomable mystery? It's fortunate for us that we don't need to know. We do need to be willing to step aside and allow it to happen.

That our hearts would call out for the light and love of God is no mystery in and of itself. Having been created in and with that same Light and that same Love the heart calls for that which is completion and fulfillment. It calls for that which provides clarity, perspective and strength in sweet vulnerability. Where to begin?

Become aware of your personal heart-call. Among all of your must, can and future do's, sit quietly listening to what your heart needs from you. Take a walk through your neighborhood. The smallest flower is grand by design. Each vein of every petal is there with intent and purpose. Allow your heart to speak to you and when you do, allow the answer to follow.

Just as the small flower is grand by design with each piece there for purpose and intent, so is it with human beings. We are the Love of God by design. Our intent and purpose is only to extend the Love that is so freely wrapped around our lives.

Breathe in the light through which we are seen and reflect it outward toward everyone and everything you touch. Your heart will be filled with the unfathomable mystery of resting in peace and cradled in Love.

> *There is no fear in love. But perfect love drives out fear, because fear has to do with punishment. The one who fears is not made perfect in love.*
>
> 1 John 4:18–19

Take a Moment to Listen:

Sweet child of heaven, you are as you were created. Just as the moment when Love first breathed spirit into your heart, your heart longs to remember and to feel once again the fullness of completion. More and deeper will you sense who you are to Who created your very being as you let go of apprehension and allow the richness of your inheritance to fill your soul.

Guided Meditation

We are invited to participate in the relationship that began from our very creation. The fullness of divine Love, joy and gratitude is our inheritance from the space of our very creation.

Find a quiet space and relax. Breathe in deeply and exhale. Breathe in again deeply and exhale. The mystery of our relationship with our Creator is only a mystery when attempting to qualify or quantify it. Breathe in deeply again and exhale.

There is no mystery in a 'mystic'. There is however, honesty, truthfulness and total trust in an undefined relationship that has been ours from our very beginning. This cannot be reasoned, qualified or quantified. It can only be experienced. This is called 'mystical' because the mystery of the depth of love between creator and created cannot be reasoned or logically attended to. It is the mystery of reciprocally experiencing the depth of a relationship without explanation.

You not only have the ability to feel and experience the love of your Creator, but are also able to extend that love to all you touch within your day-to-day life. Sit with God and soak in the indefinable and filling love and gentleness from which you were created. It is freely given. Receive it freely and extend it as such.

Your Thoughts/Experience:

> "My Lord God, I have no idea where I am going. I do not see the road ahead of me. I cannot know for certain where it will end. . ..Therefore I will trust you always though I may seem to be lost and in the shadow of death. I will not fear, for you are ever with me, and you will never leave me to face my perils alone."
>
> Thomas Merton

Pure trust in that which is unseen may seem to be a precious commodity in this time of instant gratification, social media, show me, I can prove it to you, facebook, youtube video, instagram society that whirls faster around us each day like a vortex of social refuse. Societal acceptance, indeed its embrace of the available kaleidoscope of opportunities we are presented with in order to form basic relationships is astounding, given the face that upon occasion, it is the same accepting society that capriciously condemns the usage of those same social management tools. We continually place our trust in a capricious society though, just as we so readily trust the many forms of electronic relationships which pander to our need for community—albeit at a distance.

Electronic relationships and electronic communities do not require any level of human vulnerability or trust basic to human relationships. While we are safe from vulnerability and safe from developing trust, we are also safe from experiencing deep and lasting relationships that require both vulnerability and trust. We then are well on our way to making ourselves safe even from God.

> "But blessed is the one who trusts in the Lord, whose confidence is in him. They will be like a tree planted by the water that sends out its roots by the stream. It does not

> fear when heat comes; its leaves are always green. It has no worries in a year of drought and never fails to bear fruit."
>
> *Jeremiah 17:7-8*

Take a Moment to Listen:

Precious child, you are the light of heaven itself, and the glory of the Love of the Father. He who breathed life into your spirit, wraps you in sweet embrace delighting always in your rediscovery of the depths of your very being. Child, there is no space where Love could not dwell within you. Breathe in all that you are and were created to be and know that you cannot and will never walk the pathway alone.

Guided Meditation

We experience darkness within our relationships, within our thinking and within ourselves personally. The absence of understanding or of trust in any of those relationships invites darkness and confusion to fill that absence of understanding and trust.

Find a comfortable space in which to relax. Breathe in deeply and exhale. Fill your lungs with sweet air and blow that air into the world. Allow yourself to feel the unconditional peace that surrounds you. Breathe in that peace. This peace can and will begin to dissipate the confused sense of darkness.

Take in another breath of peace and allow it to fill your heart and touch your hungry spirit. Let yourself hear how God loves you. Listen for Him to tell you that this divine love is a surety no matter how uncertain you feel, or the world presents itself to you. His guidance is always sure.

Sit in that Love allowing it to surround and embrace you. You are loved totally and completely without reservation without judgment. Darkness cannot exist within this Love.

This Love is your home. You can never walk this world alone, for you are loved for exactly the person you are.

LOVE, GOD

Your Thoughts/Experience:

> "God defines himself as 'I am who I am', which also means: My being is such that I shall always be present in every moment of becoming."
>
> *Hans Urs Von Balthasar*

Dancing from the past to the present and back again to a fleeting now, even if in ballet shoes, has never brought us peace. Peace cannot be found in what happened then, or the myriad imaginings of what might happen later.

Still, we leap into the past, or spring into the future, our hearts held high in the air as we fear a disgraced fall. We live in our minds between constant worry or regret, either heartache or disgrace. Neither past nor future is a home we can abide. It is not a space that invites us to stay. How could it be? We were created for so much more.

God not only dwells in the present of every moment, but He invites us to dwell in the present with trust. Can we not ask Him as His child to correct our past mistakes, and somehow lead us in love to a kinder future? Does He not want the best for His child?

It is we who forget how great a love He has for each of us. It is we who forget that in each present moment, He would guide us with absolute love and tenderness. So we can safely hold his hand knowing our guidance is as sure as his unending unconditional love.

> "Do not worry about tomorrow; tomorrow will care of itself."
>
> *Matthew 6:34*

Take a Moment to Listen:

Fear my child, is a paper tiger you gaze upon when you live outside of this instant. The future is filled with images, all of which seem to captivate your frightened mind. You do not need to frighten yourself, as my peace is already yours. Gaze instead upon me in this moment, as you see me gaze upon you. Stay with me in each sacred moment where I will whisper what your heart so longs to hear. You are my precious child forever.

All you need do is call me. My love is sure. Trust in my love for you and let me guide you in each moment. Trust in my guidance. It is as sure as the sunrise each morning, for you are loved more than a thousand suns.

Guided Meditation

Close your eyes and take a deep breath as you begin to remember God's constant presence. Imagine in your mind you are surrounded by nature. Perhaps you can imagine an old, beautiful tree with gnarled, fat branches twisting upwards. Rest your eyes on the perfection of that tree. Notice the colorful birds resting at the top of the branches. There is a small brook running nearby. Try and hear the bubbling water as it bounces from the rocks and pebbles, perfect in its design.

Sit down under the tree and relax. Breathe in the peace that you find here. In that peace God speaks to you of His love. Try and hear Him. What does it feel like to hear Him tell you that He loves you? Can you accept His love for you?

Is there something that concerns you? Would you like God's guidance? Ask God to help you. Ask Him for his loving guidance. Notice if you see, hear or feel anything in response. Perhaps you will have a thought or idea that hadn't occurred to you before. If not do not worry. Try and trust that god will help guide you in a way that is personal and understandable to you. Know that this lovely place is yours to come to whenever you need God's peace.

Deborah J. Simmons-Roslak & Linda J. Orber

Your Thoughts/Experience:

"Laughter is the closest thing to the grace of God"

Karl Barth

Not knowing otherwise, we can imagine heaven to be a state of continuous joy. Here, in the midst of perfect love, our two feet are firmly planted in the ever present now. The past is gone and eternity is lived in each precious moment. Fear has dissipated. There is only safety and love so joy is ever present.

In those moments of joy and laughter, we too are totally present. The past and future have faded and we are focused on the blessing we behold in this moment. As we breathe this moment, we love and are loved by all who share this blessing. We live in an instant of total delight.

Those moments can be made manifest so much more often, if we can learn to live in the richness of where we are now. Love embraces and enfolds us. What have we to fear? If we can let go of the perceived past, and stop fearing each imagined future, we can then find delight in life itself.

Laughter comes freely when fear is gone, for love and joy are always joined as one. As we take the Hand of Love Itself, fear disappears and joy is ours once again. Heaven is now, and we are delighted by God's enormous heart, and those around us whose hands we hold.

> *"I have told you this so that my own joy may be in you and your joy complete. This is my commandment: love one another, as I love you."*
>
> *John 15:11–12*

Take a Moment to Listen:

Joy my child is my gift to you, for you were created in perfect love, and in your creation the angels sang songs of happiness and delight. I look upon you in endless joy, in every moment. If you understood the love with which you are truly known, you would never be afraid. You could never be afraid, for you would know all of heaven watches over you in delight. Let go my child of your fears, for they are nothing of permanence, nothing of substance. Let your past go and put your future into my loving hands. Allow yourself to feel the joy of heaven, and take delight in the world around you.

Laughter is indeed a grace that is yours, for joy is a taste of heaven. Delight in the love of those around you, for they too are loved and loving them is also your joy.

Guided Meditation

Sometimes we forget how much we live in past events, or the depth of our fear of the future. We forget that happiness is found in the present moment of our life. Sit quietly and take a deep breath. Breathe in deeply and exhale completely.

Think about your day. Try to remember how often you lived in a state of worry or regret. Can you see yourself in that worried state? How has it hampered you? Have you spent the day regretting decisions you have made? How much of the day have you been really present?

Now think about one moment that gave you joy. Did you notice what it was? Were you totally present in that moment? What about that moment made you so happy?

Can you take that moment of joy and imagine extending it outward, so joy extends on and on? Imagine that joyous moment shared with God. Can you allow yourself to connect with Him and share your joy with Him? Sit with God for awhile in that shared state of joy. Let yourself feel His love for you and His delight in your happiness. He wants you to be happy and filled with joy. He wants you to live without worry or regret. Take as much time as you need. There is no hurry.

Try to remember as you go through your day that God delights in your happiness and desires that you share your joy. Remember that whenever you begin to become fearful of the future or stuck in the past God will help you live in the joyous moment. All you need do is ask, for He is already there.

Your Thoughts/Experience:

> "Where can we go to find God if we cannot see Him in our own hearts and every living being?"
>
> *Swami Vivekananda*

In a moment of contemplative silence, we intently turn inward and away from the noise and distraction of the world. In this sacred moment the wonder and awe of Divine Love enfolds us in safety, and acceptance reaffirming the divinity of all the created.

This sacred Love can never be unknown quite the same way again, for we know with certainty it is there and that it is only ego choice which asks that we pretend not to know, or question its existence. We know that Love can never leave us, for it breathes life into every fiber of our being.

As Love breathes life into every fiber of our being, so does that same Love flow within our sisters and brothers, binding us together as one expression of wholeness and divinity within creation.

Could we deny the existence of our arm or leg? Yet this we try when we deny the wholeness and holiness of our brothers and sisters. When our sisters and brothers are filled with fear and have forgotten to look deeper into their hearts, we can be reminders that if Love lives within us, it must also dwell inside of all. We remind them with our kindness, and compassion that Love indeed lives.

> "Do you not know that you are a temple of God, and that the Spirit of God dwells in you?"
>
> *1 Corinthians 3:16*

Take a Moment to Listen:

In the quiet of your heart you will find me, for here I live within you. Love surrounds your heart, and encompasses your soul. You need not react to a brother or sister's fear, my child. You merely need to join with me in love, for fear lives in darkness, and the light of my love will dispel all darkened shadows.

Join with me in love, and together we will calm the fears of those that are yet afraid. Together, we will open their hearts once again to the glorious light of love.

Guided Meditation

There are moments when we forget that Love is always with us. There are moments of ambivalence when we choose empty promises of fear, while knowing still, and with certainty that we are never alone and without Love.

Close your eyes and breathe in deeply. Exhale completely. Breathe in again deeply filling every part of your body. Exhale completely and while you do exhale all of the noise and distractions of the world around you until not even it's faint clamor can be heard.

Hear the quiet. Rest in this peace without boundary, without restraint. Will yourself deeper into that boundless peace, until not even your breath can be felt or heard.

Feel God's presence with you. Can you feel His love surround you and enfold you? Take your time. Allow yourself to feel how loved you are. Allow yourself to feel that love deep within your own heart. He is here with you. He is always with you. Take your time. Experience His love for as long as you need to.

When you are finished, take His love with you into the world. The world needs His love and it is yours now to extend.

Your Thoughts/Experience:

> *"You may call God love, you may call God goodness. But the best name for God is compassion."*
>
> *Meister Eckhart*

Many grew to adulthood having internalized an Old Testament god: angry, vengeful, carefully keeping a record of grievances and trespasses. This is a god of retribution. This is a god who incites terror inside the hearts of many. Gingerly, we may tip toe around this god hoping that our small endeavors might find a bit of grace. We offer an olive branch every now and again to this fear inducing god believing however, that our efforts are but shrunken and withered against an almighty fire breathing deity. We fully expect a god who condemns, punishes and revels in vengeance with a mighty hand and a mighty list full of our own faults, and shortcomings.

Where then is there space for Unconditional Love? Where then is the God of which many have spoken and taught of? Jesus, for one, showed us what Love looked like, though we never believe that level of love should or ever could apply to ourselves. We can only see with fear and trepidation.

However, what if God does not sit on a throne of angry judgments, but instead looks only with unconditional love and compassion upon all of creation? What if God who is Love only knows love, and that Love is what is given freely and without reservation? What if God who is compassion, acts only with the utmost tenderness, as a perfect parent loves a child?

Perhaps we are less fearful of punishment, than we are of such an all encompassing, unconditional Love. Perhaps what we fear the most is the depth and breadth of such glorious mercy and compassion. Perhaps we have been mistaken all along. Therein lay our salvation.

> *"What is your opinion? If a man has a hundred sheep and one of them goes astray, will he not leave the ninety-nine in the hills and go in search of the stray? And if he finds it, amen, I say to you, he rejoices more over it than over the ninety-nine that did not stray. In just the same way, it is not the will of your heavenly Father that one of these little ones be lost."*
>
> Matthew 18:12-14

Take a Moment to Listen:

There is absolutely no fear in absolute Love my child, and therefore nothing love needs to defend. Love is neither offended, nor defensive. Love never sits in superior judgment. It is only fear that seeks to elevate itself. If there is no fear in Love, then all the things you fear are your own imaginings.

I offer my hand to you—always. You are loved far more than you could ever possibly imagine. You are precious, and deeply loved now and for all eternity.

Guided Meditation

There are moments when it is difficult to imagine the depth of God's Love for each and every one of us. There are moments when we feel we don't deserve such an incredible Love, but God is insistent—His Love is ours. Each precious child is Loved, without measure and without restraint. Find a comfortable place and let yourself relax. Take a deep and filling breath.

When you are ready, invite God to be with you. It's an invitation He is always happy to accept. If there was a time you recently, or in the past felt unworthy of Love, tell Him. Let Him know what it was and how you felt. Feel free to let Him know anything that might be stopping you from accepting His healing and peace.

Let yourself hear Him tell you of His love for you. Hear Him offer you his healing peace. Give yourself permission to take the love He is offering you, and sit with Him for a while, in the safety of that Love.

Your Thoughts/Experience:

> "We need to find God, and he cannot be found in noise and restlessness. God is the friend of silence. See how nature—trees, flowers, grass—grows in silence; see the stars, the moon, and the sun, how they move in silence . . . We need silence to be able to touch souls."
>
> *Mother Teresa*

We inhabit a world full of need to dos, want to dos, gadgets, electronics and constant stimulation both outward and inward. We live in spaces where the television is blaring, cell phones are never turned off and devices are activated as if our lives depended upon their existence. We become conditioned to respond immediately to noise and input, almost as though we have become dependent on stimulation as a distraction. This distraction can be a way of not turning inward and looking into our own hearts.

Somewhere inside of our quiet, deep thought we know it is in that silence that we discover a deeper love. It is within silence that we discover we are loved. It is in silence that we discover Love itself.

This is the beauty of nature, that we can feel the profound in the quiet. We can feel gentleness and beauty and Love itself. These are all the gifts that tenderly wait in our own heart, if we have the courage to look.

> "Do not store up for yourselves treasures on earth, where moth and decay destroys, and thieves break in and steal. But store up treasures in heaven, where neither moth nor decay destroy, nor thieves break in and steal. For where your treasure is, there also will your heart be."
>
> *Matthew 6:19–21*

Take a Moment to Listen:

Accumulation of things and stimulation of the world will usually leave you empty my child, for that which clangs or distracts could never satisfy a far deeper need. As you encounter that which I have created, the recognition sparks joy, for you recognize your own joyful creation. Creation is expansive and glorious and filled with a love that cannot be contained. Each time you encounter creation with wonder, you acknowledge the Mystery of Love itself. Each time you open your heart to a greater love, allowing yourself to be touched by my presence, you allow yourself to be held for a moment in love's embrace. It is in that silent, holy moment that you feel whole. It is this moment that you will forever carry in your heart.

Guided Meditation

We can easily look around our homes and find ourselves surrounded by meaningless stuff just as we can hear the constant noise of one sort of media or another. Let's take a moment to focus on something more meaningful, and that will give us peace.

Close your eyes and breathe deeply. Exhale completely and breathe in deeply again. In your mind's eye, place yourself in small woodland. You know this place. You have walked by every tree, and through the flowering brush. You have watched the birds overhead and smiled at their exquisite flight.

Sit down in your favorite spot. You know just where it is. Put your back against your favorite tree. Here you can revel at the endless carpet of sculpted grasses and plant life. The smell of spring soil and new growth tickle your nose as the sun overhead gently shines with warmth and light.

You feel a new breeze licking your face as you hear the heartfelt songs of winged creatures around you. Allow yourself to experience the joy of here and right now. Allow yourself to soak in the peace and balance of where you are.

In this space, allow yourself to feel the presence of God. He is there with you. If you choose, you can tell Him what ever is on your mind. You can listen for His loving answer.

Allow yourself to feel His boundless love for you. You can take this Love with you now, wherever you go. Rest for a while in this sacred space.

Your Thoughts/Experience:

> "On the parable of the Good Samaritan: I imagine that the first question the priest and Levite asked was: if I stop to help this man, what will happen to me? But by the very nature of his concern, the Good Samaritan reversed the question: if I do not stop to help this man, what will happen to him?"
>
> *Martin Luther King Jr.*

Placing a stranger's concerns before our own is certainly not the norm for the majority. A glance at the evening news, a newspaper or breaking social media will confirm that a person other than ourselves (or those in our deemed group) is unlike and therefore part of 'the others' (who is every one else not in our deemed group).

It is the ego that loves to look out for itself, caring only for its own survival. When our ego is in the drivers seat, no one could possibly matter. True to itself—the ego is hell bent on condemning all those that are not 'it'. The ego loves to bask in its' own preconceived sense of superiority and rightness. It feeds and grows from its sense of smugness and self-righteousness. The ego lives a life of: me versus you as it sits on a precarious throne of hatred. The parable of the Good Samaritan turns the ego upside down on its proverbial head. When love is the driving force, other people (anyone not yourself) matters. Love looks at a stranger with compassion, because Love sees no enemies. Everyone then, is a brother or sister. Love looks upon another and sees its own self.

Imagine a world where Love is the driving force and fear merely takes a back seat. Perhaps we can let fear off at the next crossroads—and tell it to take a hike.

> "... A man fell victim to robbers as he went down from Jerusalem to Jericho. They stripped and beat him and went off leaving him half-dead. A priest happened to be going down that road, but when he saw him, he passed by on the opposite side. Likewise a Levite came to the place, and when he saw him, he passed on the opposite side. But a Samaritan traveller who came upon him was moved with compassion at the sight. He approached the victim, poured oil and wine over his wounds and bandaged them. Then he lifted him up on his own animal, took him to an inn and cared for him. The next day he took out two silver coins and gave them to the innkeeper with the instruction, 'Take care of him. If you spend more than what I have given you, I shall repay you on my way back.' Which of these three, in your opinion, was a neighbor to the robbers' victim?"
>
> He answered, "The one who treated him with mercy." Jesus said to him, "Go and do likewise."
>
> Luke 10:30-37

Take a Moment to Listen:

Division could never be from Love, my child, but is always from the ego, for the ego manifests fear. It is fear that produced division, and ugly walls we feel then feel a need to build. There is no fear in Love, for it sees itself in everything. Every child is lovely. Do not allow your ego to cleverly mask what is right in front of you. Instead, ask me to help you to see with clarity.

Love is always humble and always kind. If you are seeing hatred and division, then you are seeing through darkened glasses. If you are not sure, listen with your heart. It is your heart that will always guide you to love and love will always guide you to me.

Guided Meditation

We are so often fearful of groups of people who are unlike us. Perhaps they are from a different social group, economic group, or speak a different language or dress differently. It can be easy to forget the world is filled with individuals, all of whom are loved in the eyes of God.

Sit in a comfortable place. Close your eyes and take a deep breath in. Exhale completely, and breathe in deeply once again. In your mind's eye place yourself on a grassy slope. Allow your self to look down and survey the field below. You can clearly see from your spot. Invite God to be in the lovely place with you. Take time to feel His presence with you.

Now look down and notice a small crowd of people below. At first, they are a group of people wearing clothes you are not familiar with and speaking a language you cannot understand. Now look closely. Each person is an individual. Do you see that?

Can you notice a couple leaning close into one another? Do you see a parent with a child? Can you see grandparents holding the hand of their grandchild?" Watch how they laugh with one another, the easy way they convey to one another much the same emotions you have felt yourself. Do you notice the apparent love they share with one another? Perhaps the group you were afraid of is not so different from you.

Ask God to help you see the love He has for each of them. Then, ask God to help you to feel the Love he has for you. Can you feel that Love is no different for one than another?

Stay in this lovely spot for a while longer. When you are ready to leave, take His love with you.

Your Thoughts/Experience:

> "Constant kindness can accomplish much. As the sun makes the ice melt, kindness causes misunderstanding, mistrust, and hostility to evaporate."
>
> *Albert Schweitzer*

An instant of kindness with its compassion and gentleness can touch a heart that is desperate for healing. Like an unexpected gentle spray of water on a forgotten and wilted flower kindness can energize, heal and bless those that are in need.

There was a time, when a young boy was in the hospital. He went through a battery of tests for a week. His mother slept restlessly on a small cot next to him. During the day a parade of doctors, nurses and various professions came into his room. They would proceed to ask his mother a litany of questions, all seemingly useless. After a few days of this routine, the child's mother was tired, emotionally wrung out and overwhelmed.

She left her son's room, wandered into the hospital corridor and slid down the wall on to the floor, where she stayed slumped. Out of nowhere a member of the clergy appeared. He asked if he might join her, and then proceeded to sit next to her on the floor of that busy hallway.

They talked for a while. They prayed together. He then left. She never did find out this man's name or the denomination of his religion, but she always remembered that gracious act of kindness.

It was a compassionate, lovely gesture that helped her feel that she too mattered. His gesture lifted her spirit, it allowed her space to take a breath. In all of the weariness of those first few days, for the first time she didn't feel alone. She had been given nourishment in a time of dryness. It was as though someone greater than herself was reminding her that there is love and concern in the world and that she was entitled to it. It was an unforgotten act of graciousness.

Every act of kindness is a reminder of a greater Love. We are not only part of that Love, but we stand in for that glorious Love. Every act of kindness we bestow is a reminder of Who created us, and that Love—His Love lives inside of us.

> "A friend owes kindness to one in despair, though he have forsaken the fear of the Almighty."
>
> Job 6:14

Take a Moment to Listen:

Love will envelop you in kindness and lift your heart to mine. My love is always gentle and full of tenderness. As you walk the world with your hand in mine, look upon your sisters and brothers with gentleness, for they often live in fear and sorrow and have forgotten the love that surrounds them.

When you see a brother or sister in pain, give the same tenderness as I forever give to you. As you remind them of that gracious love that lives within you, you remind yourself as well, for love is a never ending circle of gentleness and peace that will reflect back to you the joy that lives within your heart.

Guided Meditation

Find a quiet place and close your eyes. Relax as you take a deep breath. Can you remember an act of kindness that was graciously given to you? What was it? Can you recall how that act of kindness affected you? Think about this for a while. Was there a time you were spontaneously kind to another? Can you recall that particular incident? What was it like? How did that interaction make you feel?

Sit with that feeling for a while. How did your own act of kindness affect you? Did it help you to remember a Greater Love? Sit with that Love now. Sink into it and allow yourself to feel how loved you are—by Love Itself. Sit in that space for as long as you need to sit.

As you go about your day, try to recall from time to time that feeling of being loved. As you try and recall how being kind affected you perhaps, it will help you to repeat that kindness to those around you.

Your Thoughts/Experience:

"The function of prayer is not to influence God, but rather to change the nature of the one who prays"

Kierkegaard

Parking places have become sacred spaces for which people formulate their most heartfelt entreaties. Like the flight of monarch butterflies, prayers soar by the thousands between the days of Monday and Friday during early morning arrivals or mid-day movements.

"Please God, just one space so I'm not late for work. I don't even mind walking a few blocks, please oh please. I'll even try to be a better person today if only. . ."

And so the entreaty swirls around a want and perceived need based upon a future fear deposited in the present. What is forgotten within this energetic exercise is the meaning of communication between the Loved and the Beloved and the nature of Divine immutable Love.

The parking space prayer assumes a god who can be cajoled, bargained with and who might listen if we just find the key words to mumble. Unfortunately, our parking space prayer also assumes a god who is capricious, possibly withholding, and who can at any point somehow pick up all of his marbles and disappear from the prayer game.

Should we miraculously find a parking spot, we thank this god profusely, tell everyone how god must've heard and answered. How very blessed we feel—for the moment. Should we get a traffic ticket on that same day, all blessed feelings are off. We are angry with this little god of our own making, and we are back to square one in our journey of communication with the Divine.

LOVE, GOD

> *"And if we know that he hears us—whatever we ask—we know that we have what we asked of him."*
>
> 1 John 5:15

Take a Moment to Listen:

As your heart was molded by my own, there is no need for words or wishes in order to be heard and felt. Your fears are allayed in the shelter and comfort of my heart, which is also your own. In moments of anxiety or fear, know that all passes away except for the love that has created you and from which you were formed. Be sure in the blessed nature of your heart. Be sure in our love that is your heritage, and which flows unimpeded by the distractions and noise of form and confusion. You are simply my own as I am yours. Be at peace.

Guided Meditation

Communication is a form of communing, which by itself has no specific form, format or even words necessarily. Communication or communing with Divine Love needs nothing but a willing mind and an open heart.

Make yourself comfortable. Close your eyes. Breathe in deeply. Exhale slowly and completely. Breathe in again filling your lungs and then exhale slowly emptying them. Feel your heart open. Breathe in deeply again. As you exhale feel your heart open still more.

In your mind's eye, place yourself in an open space and look upward. All before you is deep black sky without end and no delineated beginning.

Divine Love is. It surrounds you and stretches into the deep and limitless sky. You can feel a slight wind shift as a puff of air brushes your cheek. Safe. You are safe within this formlessness. Peace holds you as your heart opens wider.

You are flooded with gratitude and joy and a love that is deeper than the sky above you. Stay with this feeling allowing it to fill every cell in your body.

You are loved completely just as you are. Your heart knows this—listen to its song.

Your Thoughts/Experience:

"I don't know what your destiny will be, but one thing I know: the only ones among you who will be really happy are those who will have sought and found a way to serve."

Albert Schweitzer

At one time or another as children, we repeatedly have misplaced items that mattered to us: our homework, our gloves, our library card. As adults, the list often got longer: our keys, our wallet, or the glasses unknowingly perched on top of our head. Happiness however, is not a noun that can be easily misplaced—yet it often eludes us, as if it were simply hiding. We spend our busy lives believing that the key to our happiness lies in what we obtain. Showing off a grander house, a luxury car, or believing if we exude just the right image, we somehow have the answer to feeling fulfilled. Yet we know how quickly the excitement of *that* disappears. The emptiness rolls in like a dull fog—and we are restless for something else. We rarely suspect that happiness was never hiding there.

What we fail to notice is that when we open ourselves up to giving or serving in any capacity, we nurture a warm quiet joy that radiates in our heart. Even as we remember what it felt like to humbly serve another—we can still bask in that moment of joy.

We sometimes secretly envy those we know who graciously give their time and gifts, and wonder why we don't do more of the same. But as quickly as that thought comes, it passes just as quickly. We imagine the answer is in some fancy product we need that would magically produce a lasting change.

If only we can remember that it is in the service of love in any capacity, which has the ability to produce true fulfillment that is eternal. It is a lesson that once learned and remembered, can become a lifetime of quiet joy. We were all given gifts to share, and it is in that gracious sharing that our hearts finally feel welcomed home.

> "The greatest among you will be the one who serves the rest. Whoever exalts himself shall be humbled, but whoever humbles himself shall be exalted."
>
> Matthew 23:11–12

Take a Moment to Listen:

There is nothing that can fill your heart, my child, outside of love. For nothing else is worthy of a beloved child of God. Do not look to false grandeur, which can never touch your lovely heart. It is not where lasting fulfillment lives. Look instead to the love deep inside, that we share as one. That is what is worthy to be given and received. Every child of God has been given cherished gifts, which are given to be shared. It is in that sharing that your heart will gratefully soar. For this is what divine love created you to do, and this is Love's lasting gift to you, to be extended in generosity and joy.

Guided Meditation

We often look in the wrong place to find what makes us happy. It is as if we are playing hide and go seek, except happiness is not hiding. We are merely seeking in empty spaces. Close your eyes and take a deep breath. Think about something that you really wanted to purchase. Can you remember how it felt when you got it? Notice how long those feelings lasted.

Now think about something you did for someone else. Can you think of a time you shared something, or went out of your way for someone? What was that like?

How did that make you feel? Can you notice how the other person felt that you shared with? Now notice the difference in the fleeting joy of getting an object, and the joy of having given or shared.

Perhaps you would like to find more opportunities to feel those feelings of joy again in giving. Talk to God about that and ask Him to help you.

Your Thoughts/Experience:

> *"The tragedy of the world is not that men do not know God; the tragedy is that, knowing Him, they still insist on going their own way."*
>
> William Barclay

The history of justification is as old as the history of humankind. It's a competitive sport with those who are particularly gifted in its dark art. They rise to the top of successful business across the spectrum of moneymaking interests supposing that karma or entitlement has gracefully led them there. Perhaps that is true with some, but with others it was the carefully built layers of justification, which allowed them such gratis, even as they stepped upon the heads and faces of others as they climbed.

For novice players, there are certainly a variety of justification home edition games to play with your spouse, family or just a group of friends.

Sharpen your skills with Justify! It's the game where you invent explanations for sour intent, malicious motivation and negative behavior toward others (and yourself). The rules are fairly simple:

At no time are you to look inward and take responsibility for actions both positive and negative.

When called into account for seemingly negative behavior, begin to build an explanation, which confuses your listener, and causes her or him to doubt their initial reaction.

Practice your explanation until every inch of you truly believes what you have fabricated.

Advance forward as many steps as you are able and wait for the next round of play.

Love, God

> *"Many are the plans in a person's heart, but it is the Lord's purpose that prevails."*
>
> Proverbs 19:21

Take a Moment to Listen:

Free will allows you to choose in every moment that which you will think, take action upon and believe. It is a choice and it is your own however, when not used in conjunction with divine will, can only lead you further away from the love that to you endlessly. The choices that you make without benefit from the reflection of your heart will not and could not benefit you or your brothers and sisters. Justifying the actions of a little, and divided will can only satisfy an immediate perceived need informed by a belief in lack both personally and of the Hand of Love.

In Truth there cannot be a lack of love from the Creator of Love itself for any child. In Truth your free will is given so that you may freely choose to join in the song of eternal love your creator sings for you and for all of beloved creation.

Guided Meditation

Find a comfortable place and relax. Take a deep breath. Exhale slowly. Become aware of what you choose to focus upon. What are you focused upon as you take another deep breath? Exhale completely.

What you choose to focus upon is either the choice made with a little will, or a choice that is freely made in conjunction with Love's Will. Breathe in again deeply and exhale. The Will of Divine Love calls you to choose to join in the song of Love, Creativity, Expansion and Acceptance. Breathe in deeply and as you do, feel the pull to Divine Love that calls to you. Exhale completely.

For as long as you can, sit with the knowledge of choice that all of creation shares. We can choose with our small and divided will, or we can choose with The Will of Divine Love, which connects and enfolds all the created.

Your Thoughts/Experience:

> "Where can we go to find God if we cannot see Him in our own hearts and every living being."
>
> Swami Vivekananda

In a moment of contemplative silence, we shut out all the noise of the world. Here in a sacred moment, we can recognize with wonder and awe, the Love that is nestled deep within our own hearts. That sacred love can never be unknown again—for we know with certainty it is there. We know Love can never leave us. It lives in us, and beats within our own hearts.

It is only natural then, to extend that love to every living being. As we know Love lives forever in us, it must live in the hearts of our brothers and sister. Even when they are filled with fear, we can recognize that they have forgotten to look deeper. We can look on them with the love and compassion they have forgotten. We remind them that if Love lives in us, it must also live in them. We remind them with our loving kindness that Love indeed lives.

> "Do you not know that you are a temple of God, and that the Spirit of God dwells in you?"
>
> 1 Corinthians 3:16

Take a Moment to Listen:

In the quiet of your heart you will find me. For here I live in you. Love surrounds your heart, and encompasses your soul. You need not react to a brother or sister's fear my child. You merely need to join with me in Love, for fear lies in darkness and the light of my love will dispel all darkened shadows. Join with me in love, and together we will calm the fears of those that are afraid. Together we will open their hearts one again to the glorious light of Love.

Guided Meditation

Sometimes we forget that Love is always with us. When we have found the love inside of us, we can know with certainty that we are never alone.

Close your eyes and take a deep breath. Try and shut out all the noise outside of you. Imagine the noise seems to be further and further away. Try and feel how very quiet it is. Notice how peaceful you begin to feel. Can you allow yourself to go deeper into that peace?

Feel God's Presence with you. Can you feel His love surround you and enfold you? Take your time. Let yourself feel how loved you are. Let yourself feel that love deep within our own heart. He is here with you. He is always with you. Take your time and experience His love for as long as you need to.

When you are done take His love with you into the world. The world needs His love and it is yours now to share.

Your Thoughts/Experience:

> "I do not dispute with the world; rather it is the world that disputes with me."
>
> *Gautama Buddha*

Rambling through some 25,550 or so days of existence attempting to bend the wills of those around us is exhausting. Still, we stand smugly confident with our knowing and understandings. We believe our answers are correct, our actions proprietary, our words succinct. If only others could see what we see, and know what we know. Our perspective is the right one. People ought to listen. Sound familiar?

Everything from bureaucratic agencies to social mores, politics and policies could benefit, we believe by operating with a few twists and changes from our point of view. While in some instances, this may hold an amount of truth, what is clearly true is our struggle with the world at large and the people who inhabit it. Through our judgment filled thoughts we know what is best for everything and everyone. Our judgments molded by past experiences and swayed by certainty of what may come enslave us between an ever present yesterday and tomorrow. The continuous present is given no expression, while we feel exhausted, and resentful of what and whom we have surrounded ourselves.

> "That is why every one of you who judges another is inexcusable. By your judgment you convict yourself, since you do the very same thing."
>
> *Romans 2:1*

Take a Moment to Listen:

The judgments you lay upon the world at large are but judgments against your own peace. There is order in that peace you would deny yourself, as there is clarity and the truth of Love Itself.

In stillness, judgment falls away unveiling the nature of both Loved and Beloved. You are whole and healed in this stillness. You are loved, as is all of creation is loved.

Know then, that judgment without guidance is but a wall built by fear block by block attempting to separate you from the truth of Love, as it also attempts to hold you apart from the whole of creation.

Rest in the peace and stillness shared with you from the moment of your very inception and know that in truth, Love is the only conclusion.

Guided Meditation

As adults we can be overly focused on striving for excellence, not being criticized, or maintaining some way of presenting ourselves to the world. We often forget to lose ourselves to something that we love. We have forgotten how to play.

Find your favorite quiet spot and take a deep breath. Relax into God's presence and take another deep breath. Breathe in God's love, peace and healing. When was the last time you felt lost in joy? When did you feel so engrossed in what you were doing and the joy you had in doing it- that you were unaware of time passing? Let yourself think about that honestly. If it seems like playing is rare, then why is that? What do you think has stopped you from finding more joy in your life? Are you too focused on how you will be perceived? Have you become so concerned about how something will look, that you have forgotten how to enjoy whatever task you are doing? Take your time as you look at this. Then imagine what it would be like if you felt more relaxed and less worried. What do you imagine that to be like?

As God to help you to let go of whatever fears are keeping you from having more joy in your life. Ask God to help you live more in the moment and to be less concerned about a future that hasn't appeared yet. Then sit with God in his peace and listen to whatever you think he wants you to know. Listen with an open heart.

Your Thoughts/Experience:

"The first duty of love is to listen."

Paul Tillich

Love is always open and wholly empathic. Love doesn't judge or dismiss or condemn. Love merely listens. We welcome another in love when our hearts too are open and we listen through the ears of compassion and understanding.

That being said, it is often difficult to get ourselves and our supercilious attitudes out of the way. We come to most situations and formulate solutions with our own pre-judgments and with an air of arrogance and superiority. It is impossible then to listen in empathy when justified conclusions sit in the forefront of an exchange.

Exactly what is needed before we can listen to another with openness and real empathy? We need first of all to suspend our own twisted judgments, and listen with an open heart. In this way, we are 'stepping into another's shoes' so to speak and walking in their footsteps.

What if there was no need to concern our selves with judgment, or comparison, or indignant righteousness? What if there was no need to apply a preconceived notion of hierarchy in any given exchange with another? What if we listened to understand? It is in that attempt to understand without judgment when empathy emerges and grace quietly pours in and around us. When grace and love enters, there is God, for they are one.

> "There is no fear in love. But perfect love drives out fear, because fear has to do with punishment. The who fears is not made perfect in love." John 4:18

Take a Moment to Listen:

Love, my child, will always open your heart to help heal both you and your brother and sister. My love is always accepting and gentle. There could be neither fear nor condemnation in love that is wholly present for all.

Listen with me to your brothers and sisters. Share the love that is already in your heart that is yours to heal. It will connect you to others in love and empathy, as I am always and forever connected to you.

Guided Meditation:

Find a safe and quiet spot. Sit down and take a deep breath. Exhale and breathe in deeply once again. Think of someone you do not particularly like. I am sure that person has entered your mind pretty quickly!

In your minds eye watch as they move about in their day. Perhaps they are involved in daily tasks. Feel yourself step back, just observing. Try for a moment to suspend judgment as you continue to observe. What do you know about this person's daily routines, their thoughts or how they feel about themselves when alone? Could life have been particularly difficult at one point or another? Perhaps they behave in a way that is impossible for you to fathom. Perhaps, their public beliefs are impossible to reconcile with your own.

Can you imagine what this person's life was like as a child? Could they have grown up in an oppressive situation complete with continual fear and pain? For a moment, could you see them without your preconceived anger? Can you see them through the eyes of peace? Try to sit within that peace asking God to bless them. Love sees only love and it extends to everyone.

Your Thoughts/Experience:

> *"The first step in evolution of ethics is a sense of solidarity with other human beings."*
>
> *Albert Schweitzer*

We do not journey alone. We walk this world full of other individuals who journey also. Many are frightened, or sick or homeless. Some are filled with a past that has haunted and hurt them. Many suffer pain whether it is physical, emotional or spiritual.

If we are to take seriously an evolution of ethics, it could only be with an acceptance and a knowing that each and every individual undertakes a journey that is not entirely of their own conscious making. Within this understanding we can connect to every other human being, within this understanding, we have common ground.

There is a great deal of time and energy spent on separating ourselves from groups of others. Accents, language, location and physical qualities become a reason for separation. Then there are the belief systems, customs, routines and rituals that become divisive justifications for a tiered system of ethics. Simplistically however, we are all wanderers on a journey toward home.

Imagine if the same energy that drives separateness drove connection. Imagine if we used the immense energy available to us to look past the superficial differences in order to focus on what it is that inextricably connects us one to the other in this journey we call life.

> "To his disciples, he said here are my mother and my brothers. Whoever does the will of my Father in heaven is my brother and sister and mother."
>
> *Matt: 12:50*

Take a Moment to Listen:

There is no heart pushed aside from what is its own sweet child. Love is not capricious in its abundance. There are no boundaries, nor borders that can separate Love from any part of creation. As each is totally and completely cared for, the wholeness of creation is held in holy unity. Understanding may not conceive of such wholeness, but the heart hears a familiar song and follows willingly.

Guided Meditation

Find a calm and quiet spot to sit. Take a deep breath. Exhale and breathe in and out again. Try and feel God's love surrounding you. Sit with that love for a while. Take as long as you need.

Imagine you are walking through a crowd of strangers. Everyone is in a hurry and you are not familiar with these strangers. Perhaps they make you a little anxious as their dress and movements are not something that you are accustomed to. Stop a moment and ask God to help you see these people through his eyes. Look again at those around you.

Imagine this time seeing through God's love. What is different? Can you feel your own fear and anxiety disappear as you see them as his children, whom he loves? What is this like for you? Take your time looking around and becoming more aware of what you feel. Allow the beginnings of joy to fill you, knowing these aren't strangers at all, but companions along the same journey. How does the letting go of judgment lighten the burden you've been carrying?

Look all around you and let yourself become aware of all that you are feeling. Can you allow peace to fill the space where the burden of judgment was? Sit in that peace and joy knowing that you do not journey alone. Allow the freedom and light and love to guide even your breath. Breathe it in as much as you need to.

Know that you will take all of this within you out into the world. This is who you are and what you will share with whomever paths you cross.

Your Thoughts/Experience

"The final wisdom of life requires not the annulment of incongruity but the achievement of serenity with and above it."

Reinhold Niebuhr

We are a reactive society, often swinging from one reaction to the next as if our hand is constantly on a gear stick waiting to accelerate. We react to anything and everything on full throttle as we enjoy the adrenalin rush gained by our own drama. However, none of it brings us wisdom, as we are not grounded in a calm, centered place. Rather, we rely on our gut reactions that can and do fluctuate from one moment to the next as fickle as the current wind direction.

What would it mean to sit with a sense of deep serenity? What would it be like to act from a place of wisdom, balance and healing? Maybe if we found a way to shift our mind and connect to something greater then our own small selves, we might have something to contribute that is healing. While our knee jerk reactions could not heal anything, it is the Greater Love connecting all of us that speaks wisdom to hearts in pain and chaos.

That wisdom lies within a heart that is calm in its center and filled with ever flowing peace. It is the still small voice of inner strength and quiet that speaks. This is the voice of love and gentleness.

We have learned to tune out this lovely voice by our incessant need for drama and chaos. Yet if we choose to be still for a moment, the answer and the love that we seek is already there—waiting for us to listen.

DEBORAH J. SIMMONS-ROSLAK & LINDA J. ORBER

> *"After the earthquake came a fire but the Lord was not in the fire. And after the fire came a gentle whisper.*
>
> Kings 19:12

Take a Moment to Listen:

Peace is never found outside of yourself, but within your very being. It quietly abides waiting for your choice to allow it entrance into your heart. You only need to turn inward where it dwells having never left its rightful home. When you are distracted by all the shiny objects of stimulation that keeps you stuck in a whirlwind of your own reaction, remember that there is another choice you can make.

In choosing differently, you choose to break the cycle, instead choosing the peace and love and shelter that has been given to you to both hold and share. When you are one with peace, you cannot but share it as it permeates every part of you making your presence an invitation to others.

It is for you to remember what it is that matters and why you are here. Peace waits in silence and love, for your choice.

Guided Meditation:

Find a quiet space and take some time to settle in. Take a deep breath in and then out. Is there anything that you have been preoccupied with? Have these thoughts or actions made you feel anxious?

As you breathe in and out, ask for God's peace. Make a deliberate choice. Imagine that sacred peace slowly filling your heart and mind as it quiets the anxious thoughts. Watch as those thoughts dissipate within this peace and strength.

Imagine your entire self filled with this peace. Your entire body a vessel overfilled with the peace and quiet joy of divine love. Allow it to radiate outward. Imagine walking the world radiating this peace to everyone you meet. What does this feel like?

Visualize yourself living each day passing this peace to whoever crossed your path.

Feel the fullness of gifting all with peace. Breathe deeply in and out. Stay in this space as long as you can.

Your Thoughts/Experience:

> "When we think of the idea, we do not add virtue to virtue but think of Jesus Christ, so that the standard of human life is no longer a code, but a character."
>
> E. Stanley Jones

Love is always loving, giving and emptying itself without lack of any kind. When we think of the humanity of Jesus, we think of someone who was consistently in the process of offering to another. Where there was a need, that need was met. It didn't matter whether there was not enough wine, or a deeper need for inner healing. Love walked the earth and gave and healed and helped. No one was turned away, or passed by or treated in a way that lacked dignity and compassion.

As such, the human Jesus becomes a model of humanity. The human Jesus walked the earth in gentleness, acceptance and understanding. He listened, he heard as he extended healing and hope. This is love in action, fully human.

This model of what it is to be fully human leaves us no excuse to pretend that love in action, and trust in a greater truth is not possible, because someone before us has shown the possibility.

When feeling depleted, or judgmental over our own irritating behaviors and failures that block our awareness, we have an example, a model to look toward as both inspiration and encouragement.

Should we forget, as we often do, Love will gently remind us- we are not alone on this journey. Simply make the decision to step aside and let Love lead.

Love, God

> *"Little children, we must stop expressing love merely by our words and manner of speech; we must love also in action and in truth."*
>
> John 3:18

Take a Moment to Listen:

Love, my child, is never static. It flows from heart to heart and is open to all who are thirsty. Love gives in every situation and every moment. There is no moment in time or in eternity when love could ever fail you. You need only open your heart and receive. There is nothing more for you to do, for once your heart is filled you will want to share as well, for love in truth can but share what it is.

You need never feel inadequate, or wanting, for love sees you in truth and as you are. Open your heart my child and let love flow once again through you.

Guided Meditation:

Find a space that is comfortable and settle yourself. Close your eyes and breathe in deeply. Release that breath slowly and completely. Breathe in again deeply. Focus on your breath as you slowly and completely release it. Allow yourself to feel the presence of love with you. Breathe in that love. Fill yourself with this love, allowing it to emanate through your body. Take in how loved you are and how much you are cherished. Sit with those feelings for a while.

Now imagine taking the hand of love itself—however you imagine that to be. Love is not only with you, but guiding you with every thought and every step you take if you allow it to be so.

Remember a situation which you might have had some difficulties or conflicts. It doesn't matter how small or large those situations were. Sit with that for a few moments. It's okay to feel uncertain about that situation.

Now ask love to guide you. You are holding love's hand. Ask love to help you, then quietly listen. What is love whispering to your heart? Take your time. There is no rush. Listen with your heart open. Let love guide you.

In every situation, you need only remember to ask and love will joyfully answer. How does it feel to know that there is never a limit on love's desire to help you? Allow yourself to sit with those feelings. You are never alone and or without help. All you need do is take love's hand and let yourself be led.

Your Thoughts/Experience:

> *"So then, when I speak to you I speak to myself. If I seem to warn or rebuke you, so much you as myself, to whom the warning or rebuke is addressed."*
>
> Joseph Barber Lightfoot

Oh, how we love to point fingers at everyone else. We relish picking apart the shortcomings of friends and family. Even strangers are not spared. We don't have to know people, in order to list their grievous errors. In fact, strangers are the easiest to pick apart. Yet, somehow, in all of this faultfinding we never seem to notice the same behavior in ourselves. We are so sure that we are never the ones that can be insensitive, difficult, or tirelessly defensive. We rarely reflect on our own behavior and insensitive attitudes. We automatically project our own failings outward and notice it in everyone else. It's almost like a volleyball we keep smacking over the net to the other side. We reflect very little about ourselves, yet revel in our own feelings of being a victim.

Yet, it was Jesus who said, you hypocrite, first take the log out of your own eye, and then you will see clearly to take the speck out of your brother's eye. Matt 7:5. So then, what stops us from really reflecting upon ourselves? Jesus clearly told us what to do. Why in heavens name don't we do it? Introspection is usually difficult. Introspection and reflection are a lot of work. Reflection done honestly, can be painful. It's usually hard to recognize that it is ourselves that have so many shortcomings. The idea of real reflection and change puts us in a position of taking responsibility.

Once we can recognize our own behavior and become aware—we can actually begin to be liberated. We no longer have to tirelessly and continuously smack that ball into someone else's court. We no longer have to walk the world feeling like a victim.

Deep inside we don't have to feel guilty for pointing a finger at another, knowing we have behaved in such similar ways.

If we can learn to reflect with God's love, the pain is less and the path to freedom is open. God's love does not condemn, but gently helps to free us. God is always offering us his peace. Isn't that what we all really long for?

> "Peace I leave with you: My peace I give to you: not as the world gives do I give to you. Do not let your heart be troubled, nor let it be fearful."
>
> John 14:27

Take a Moment to Listen:

Self-awareness becomes freedom my child, when you look at yourself with me. Together we will look at all your emotions and behavior with love and with kindness. There is no condemnation here. If you look gently with me, then you are holding the hand of Love itself. This will free your heart, so you will no longer have to condemn yourself or those around you. Condemnation will be replaced with love and understanding. Freedom will dwell in your heart where fear once lived. Every time you allow yourself to look with me, you are opening up a door where once you felt shackled. I will brush aside your tears and help you understand all that has happened in love and kindness. Then we will walk together and I will guide you in all that you do. Love looks upon you in joy, my child. Take my hand and walk with me. Let love help you to grow in gentleness and in peace.

Guided Meditation:

Find a calm, quiet spot and sit down. Take a couple of deep breaths. Think about the day you've had so far. Can you ask God to help you to look at your day with you? As you look at your day, was there a time that you felt particularly good about the way you responded to something? Think about that for a while. Think about how good it feels to remember when you felt good about your responsive behavior. Can you ask God to help you look at an instance when you could've done better? Can you think about what might have happened? What caused you to act the way you did? Try to be very honest with yourself. Perhaps, you are afraid of being judged somehow. If that is the case, what do you think that fear is about? Try to gently look with God's love. This is not about condemning yourself. It is about understanding. Once you can understand what you felt, ask God then to help you with whatever fear you might have had. Let him help you to heal and to see more clearly.

Your Thoughts/Experience:

> "Doubt is not the opposite of faith, it is one element of faith."
>
> Paul Tillich

Faith is not something easily kept. It seems to move in and out as we listen and believe in our chilling and disturbing fears. Sometimes we can hold on to faith like a kite in the wind and watch it soar. On other days our faith lags and drops to the hard ground with a thud. Life is hard. Faith is hard to hold on to especially on the days where the winds of life feel out of control.

What if doubt is just another element of faith, something that always comes along for the ride. You can't eliminate doubt, but you can understand it is always a part of the faith that you have. If you have faith, then you know that doubt is always there waiting for its turn to take center stage. Often you watch it, engrossed in its own performance, until you have seen enough to turn away. Then you can feel grounded again. Doubt can have an intense and fleeting performance, but it is rarely given a standing ovation and asked to return.

Faith has many elements and certainly doubt is just one, but if we can find a way not to get rattled by our doubts, and recognize it for what it is, we can hold on not just to faith but to hope as well.

The wind will come again, but when it does we don't have to feel disappointed in ourselves. Faith leads us to hope, and hope is always alive. Hope is in all the promises God has made to us. God keeps his promises. Along with hope and faith is an unconditional love that is always there for us, beyond our understanding. That love will carry us, even when our doubts feel like they are running the show. That unconditional love is greater then any doubts we could ever hold. That love will always carry us through, because it remains steadfast, unchanged and eternal, no matter how much we lose sight of its incredible unending strength.

> "We always thank God the Father of your Lord Jesus Christ, when we pray for you, because we have heard of your faith in Christ Jesus and of the love you have for all God's people-the faith and love that spring from the hope stored up in heaven and about which you have already heard in the true message of the gospel that has come to you."
>
> *Colossians 1:3-67*

Take a Moment to Listen:

Love, hope and faith surround you, and ask that you open your heart to its incredible joy. There is never a moment in time or in eternity when love would ever leave you alone in doubt. You are graced with all that love has to offer. You, my child, are asked to share in it, and know that you are never forsaken. In moments of darkness, the light of love will always and forever guide you. You need only ask. When you turn to me, my love will come rushing in to light you on your way.

You never journey alone my precious child. Doubt will come and go, but my love is eternal and is always yours. When you forget in those frightening moments, ask me to help you remember. It is always my joy to help my child remember all of the love that is theirs.

Guided Meditation:

Find a comfortable place and sit. Breathe in deeply and exhale completely. As you breathe, imagine standing by the ocean. You can hear the waves as they curl and move. Breathe in deeply and exhale completely. Smell the salty air, as you hear wave upon wave push against the shore.

Can you imagine any space where the ocean wave could not reach? Stretch your sight at the immense water that fills all spaces while lapping and extending itself further and further against the sand. Could the power of that ocean not reach into every crevice, every crag and every corner?

Such is the abundance of Divine Love, which enfolds and fills each and every heart of creation. Such is the gracious abundance of Divine Love that enfolds and fills each and every cell of your being.

Rest in the power of that Love for a while.

Your Thoughts/Experience:

> "Christianity has not been tried and found wanting: it has been found difficult and not tried."
>
> G. K. Chesterton

Jesus told us to forgive our brother seven times seventy. He asked us to love our neighbors as we would ourselves. These all seem so admirable, but often do we really put these teachings into practice, let alone live a life that fully embraces such a concept? We all love our neighbor who looks like us, or thinks like us, or has the same political views, but when it's a neighbor who looks different or thinks differently we become wary. It is so much easier to see that neighbor as 'the other', someone we don't understand or who could not possibly understand us. Our neighborhood then, becomes a little more fearful.

Then there is 'forgiveness', such a difficult concept. Why should we forgive people who don't deserve to be forgiven? We know plenty of them. We will forgive people in our family or a close friend, because we have to. The others—maybe we can hold off on forgiving them until they seem worthy of our forgiveness. On the other hand, isn't this what Jesus told us to do? We don't have to like 'the others', or hang out with them, or even have a relationship of any sort with them, but we were told to forgive them.

Maybe this forgiveness is not only for their sake, but for ours. Maybe Jesus was trying to help us to heal our own hearts in the process of forgiving our brother. If we can let go of the burden of hate and replace it with peace, imagine the healing that would follow. Putting the teachings of Jesus into practice is rather difficult. However, the result of that might just be seeing our own neighbors as a little less frightening. If we can forgive, perhaps our hearts might be a little less heavy and a little more healed. Now, wouldn't that be something?

> "And when you stand praying, if you hold anything against anyone, forgive them, so that your Father in heaven may forgive you your sins."
>
> Mark 11:25

Take a Moment to Listen:

Forgiveness is not only a gift to another, but it is always a gift to your self. It is a way to remove the fear and anger you feel and replace it with the peace of heaven. You think by forgiving, you are merely giving something away that belongs to you alone, but you are giving away is something that is hurtful, and brings you nothing you truly want. If you can open your heart just a little, the healing of heaven would heal your pain. Would you not want to walk the world filled with peace, rather then the burden you now carry?

You were meant to be loved my child, and in your pain you cannot feel what I long for you to have. Let go just the smallest bit and allow the ushering in of peace that you so deeply long for.

Guided Meditation:

Forgiveness is often difficult however you do not have to forgive by yourself. There is someone with you who loves you and wants to help you. Try and remember that forgiveness is healing for your own heart. God wants to heal you and offer you his peace instead of your pain.

Go to a comfortable spot, a place of quiet, where you can be alone. Close your eyes. Take a deep breath. Now take another. Is there someone in your life now or even in the past that you would like to work on forgiving? Think of that person. Allow yourself to have all of your feelings about them. There is no rush.

Now invite God to be with you. He wants to help you to feel more peace. As you think about this person can you let yourself think about why they may be behaving in a difficult way? Are they struggling with something that you might not have considered? We are not excusing their behavior. We are only allowing ourselves to understand. Could they possibly be driven by more fear then what you have considered? Ask God to help you understand. Perhaps underneath, they are just going through the world in a very frightened way. Perhaps you have not thought that you might have more inner strength then they have now. God loves you and wants to heal your heart. Ask him to help you understand. Then if you want, you can ask for his help in letting some of your anger and upset go. You can ask for his peace. If you are open to it, sit with that peace for a while.

Your Thoughts/Experiences:

> "We think sometimes that poverty is only being hungry, naked and homeless. The poverty of being unwanted and uncared for is the greatest poverty. We must start in our own homes to remedy this poverty."
>
> *Mother Teresa*

Fussy infants crying, toddlers throwing tantrums and elderly men and women once robust, all need assistance with simple tasks, yet the perceived constant need plays on our emotions. How irritating, frustrating and annoying all of this 'need' can be to the provider of the assistance. We find ourselves short-tempered and put upon. Sometimes it feels like the neediness never ends. Here we are with so much to do, caring for all of these difficult people. After all, there are emails to check, phone calls to make and social media participation that all need attention too. How do we stay in the loop? We end up swimming in our own frustration.

We often forget to take a step back and look at what might be going on right in front of us. That fussy baby, the tantrum throwing toddler and the elderly man and woman are frustrated as well. There is something that they feel they want to do or need to have done that creates a feeling of helplessness and anger inside of them. None of them are trying to particularly frustrate you. They are frustrated and exasperated themselves.

What if we remembered this the next time we had to deal with a family member, young or old, that seems to be annoying. Maybe they are exasperated with their own difficulties. If we could remember this, maybe we wouldn't have to back away in frustration and anger. We could see them for where they are emotionally and help give them the help they need while preserving their dignity. Perhaps that phone call we had to make could wait just a little while. Maybe we can miss social media just a little longer. Perhaps we can reconnect with someone we love and close the gap of loneliness around us. Perhaps then we could respond in compassion and understanding lifting up those we love who need our help.

> *"Be kind and compassionate to one another, forgiving each other, just as in Christ God forgave you."*
>
> Ephesians 4:32

Take a Moment to Listen:

If you can fill your heart with my love, then you would see clearly, for so many feel hurt and frustrated by their inadequacies. You could then heal their hearts by not reacting in frustration, but rather with patience, tolerance and love. There is nothing you need do, little child, but open your heart and let me reside there, for love will always heal those around you. Open your heart once again to me and let my love light the path for all those around you.

Guided Meditation:

Sit down in a comfortable spot and allow yourself to feel God's safety and peace all around you. Take a deep breath. Take another deep breath: in and out. Each time, breathe in God's love allowing it to fill you. Now ask God to be with you as you look more closely within.

With your eyes closed, think about your family and those you live with or are close to. Picture them clearly in your mind. Can you try and notice your behavior with them? How have you reacted to their anxiety or frustration? Try and notice your own behavior with them. Try and be as honest as you can. God is here to help you. Allow yourself to look inward without fear. Were there times when you could have been less frustrated or angry? How do you imagine your frustration affected them?

Think about times when you were more loving and patient. Allow yourself to see that clearly. Do you notice a difference in their reaction to your love? Do you notice how you felt when you were more loving and tolerant? Imagine what it would be like if you could be less frustrated by others, understanding that they are often frustrated by their own lack. Can you imagine how much better that feels not only for those around you, but also for yourself? Sit with that image for a while. Ask God to help you to be more aware of their frustration. Now sit with his love and take in his peace. Fill yourself with his love and patience so you can take it with you throughout your day.

Your Thoughts/Experience:

> "It is our belief that the love of possessions is a weakness to be overcome. Its appeal is to the material part, and if allowed its way, it will in time disturb one's spiritual balance. Therefore, children must early learn the beauty of generosity. They are taught to give what they prize most, that they may taste the happiness of giving."
>
> *Ohiyesa aka: Charles Alexander Eastman*

At one time or another as children, we have repeatedly misplaced items that mattered to us. It was our homework, our gloves, or our library card. As adults the list became longer: our keys, our wallet, or the glasses unknowingly perched on top of our head. Happiness however is not a noun that can be easily replaced. Yet happiness often eludes us, as if it were simply hiding. We spend our busy lives believing that the key to our happiness lies in what we obtain. As if the answer to our emptiness is having something more or something someone else could envy. That feeling of superiority doesn't last long. Emptiness rolls in like a dull fog and soon we are restless for something else. What we fail to notice is that when we open ourselves to giving or serving in any capacity, we nurture a warm quiet joy that radiates deep inside of us. We can still bask in the joy of that moment of giving or serving. If only we can remember that it is in the service of love in any capacity that produces a sense of fulfillment that is eternal. It is a lesson that once learned and remembered can lead to a lifetime of quiet joy. We were all given gifts to share. It is in that gracious sharing that our hearts are finally welcomed home.

> "The greatest among you will be the one who serves the rest. Whoever exalts himself shall be humbled, but whoever humbles himself shall be exalted."
>
> *Matthew 23:11–12*

Take a Moment to Listen:

There is nothing that can fill your heart my child, outside of love, for nothing else is worthy of a beloved child of God. Do not look to false grandeur, which can never impact your lovely heart. It is not where lasting fulfillment lives. Look instead to the love deep inside of you that we share as one. That is what is worthy to be given and received. Every child of God has been given cherished gifts that are meant to be shared. It is in that sharing that your heart will gratefully soar. This is what divine love has created you to do, and that is love's lasting gift to you.

Guided Meditation:

We often look in the wrong places to find what makes us happy. It is as if we are playing hide and go seek, but happiness is not hiding. We are merely seeking in empty places.

Close your eyes and take a deep breath. Breathe in deeply and exhale slowly. Think about something that you really wanted to buy. Can you remember how it felt when you finally got it? How long did those feelings last? Now think about something you did for someone else. Can you think of a time you shared something, or went out of your way for someone else? What was that like? How did that action make you feel? As you remember this, can you see in your mind how the person felt who received your help?

Can you begin to recognize the difference in the fleeting joy of an object and the joy of having given to another? If you like, talk to God about those feelings. Perhaps you would like more opportunities to feel that joy of giving again. As you sit quietly and think about it, ask God to help you to find more opportunities to give of your self and experience that lasting joy.

Your Thoughts/Experience:

"There is a voice that doesn't use words. Listen."

Rumi

Social media chatters on with what we suppose is important. We have electronic 'helpers' all around us as we ask them to play this or that song, or inquire as to the weather, or the latest news reports. Television gives us reality shows, endless dramatic series and comedic respites filling the air in our homes with competing sounds all designed to keep us aware, entertained and supposedly connected. Our cars are equipped with CD players and specialized radio broadcasting keeping our ears and minds occupied while going to and from wherever we need to be. Sound waves are abundant. We are busy listening, yet do not wonder why quiet is rarely a choice. We are happily distracted and largely disconnected from the deepest spaces within ourselves.

Somehow quiet is disconcerting. Our bodies react with antsy movements. We look for distractions by making a phone call, checking the email, flipping to you tube, choosing anything but quiet space. Wisdom speaks through centuries of human beings, reminding us of where our connection to one another lay; still we find a way of delaying that moment.

What exactly is the fear that stands as a doorkeeper to the awareness of our wholeness and interconnectedness with every one and every thing? The fear that demands we keep ourselves noisily busy rather then look at it square on, seeing it for what it really is. It is not a fear of the unknown; rather it is the fear of recognizing that which we truly are which keeps us imprisoned in repetitive, meaningless actions. Turn off the noise. Tune into the quiet song of your heart. There is nothing to fear.

"Your word is a lamp to my feet and a light to my path."

Psalm 119:105

Take a Moment to Listen:

Lovely child, in silence hear the call of heaven ever singing joyfully of love's creation. Your heart is but the gateway to the depths of a love that hold's your very breath as precious life. Fear not the reality of your own wholeness and holiness, for there is no fear strong enough or real enough to make untrue what has been cast by heaven itself.

Come join in heaven's song of joy, the song your heart knows well in its quiet depths. You know the way, you know the words, your love is the path and your song the direction home.

Guided Meditation:

Find a comfortable, quiet spot to sit. Close your eyes. Breathe in deeply. Exhale completely. Breathe in deeply again. Exhale completely. As you exhale, sink deeper into the noiseless space that calls you. You know the way. Sink deeper knowing that the arms of love are holding you safely.

Can you hear the call of heaven within this soundless space? This space cradles the truth of who you were created to be. Breathe in deeply. Exhale completely. The gentle strength of love's song guides you with certainty. Listen to its call of remembrance. Here you are whole. Here you are loved, as much as you are that love extended to you. Stay in this space as long as you are comfortable.

Your Thoughts/Experience:

> "The eye through which I see God is the same eye though which God sees me; my eye and God's eye are one eye, one seeing, one knowing, one love."
>
> *Meister Eckhart*

We weave in and out between the states of clarity and myopic vision, sometimes with such smooth transition that we mistake one for the other. Not that they are similar, but our perception switches without management making a clear announcement such as, "Attention: seeker of the divine, you are now operating under myopic vision therefore, take heed not to take your perceptions seriously for the next while." Wouldn't that be helpful? I think so too.

Instead, we slide in and out bumping into our own projections as well as, the projections of others formulating judgments as we go. Reacting to reactions before having had the good sense to stop and breathe for a moment will complicate matters as egos live to tango in some form of chaos or another.

Until we have use of an objective and audible operating system to assist in preventing spiritual lane changes, we need to pay attention to the state of our peace and joy, for when that is not being experienced, in the moment, we are no longer seeing through Love's eyes.

> "But the wisdom from above is first pure, then peaceable, gentle, open to reason, full of mercy and good fruits, impartial and sincere."
>
> *James 3:17*

Take a Moment to Listen:

Holy child of Love's hand, what need is there but to reach out with the same compassion that has formed your very being? What action could there be, but to love completely and totally the divine within another? As love is drawn to love so is remembrance ignited while blessings are but a breath away from your embrace.

Loving child, know that in moments of unsurety, you but turned your gaze from the source of all there is. Nothing everlasting sways in flux, nor could it. Your love is assured, your vision focused upon that which is true and real. Know that love cradles you as you journey forward.

Guided Meditation

Bring your self to your comfortable spot and sit. Take a very deep breath. Invite God to be with you. Take a few moments to feel his love and his peace surround you within your heart and in your body. Take a moment to think about a time when you felt upset about something. Perhaps you were feeling anxious, angry or afraid. Think about the emotions that went along with that situation. Take your time. Think about how you thought God saw you in those moments. Do you think he understood what you were feeling? Did you think he was trying to heal your heart? If not, then what did you think? What stopped you from allowing yourself to turn to him to experience his love and his peace? Take your time as you consider what you think might have happened. Is there something that is upsetting your peace now? Can you allow yourself to turn to him and let him heal what is upsetting you? Can you allow him to show you a different way to see the situation, or perhaps help you to just sit with him and feel wrapped in his love? Take your time as you let him help you to feel loved once again. If there is anything preventing you from allowing his help, ask him what might be getting in your way. Listen for anything you think he wants you to know. Then let yourself be filled with his peace.

LOVE, GOD

Your Thoughts/Experience:

> "Your sacred space is where you can find yourself over and over again."
>
> Joseph Campbell

Most of us long for our hard deserved vacations. We imagine ourselves on a glorious, pristine beach, or lounging by a spectacular pool as we sit atop a comfortable deck chair. Here we drift away from all of yesterday's anxieties and concerns. We imagine how truly relaxing all of this will be. But what if this isn't the only place real relaxation lays? What if we genuinely feel most relaxed when we are at home, deep within ourselves? What if we feel loved, whole and wanted whether on a gorgeous beach or a rainy sidewalk? What if where we feel whole is deep within ourselves, connected to Love Itself.

Imagine sitting in your own familiar surroundings and connecting to something that is far greater then yourself. Here is where your answers are, for here is *the answer*. Here with you, is love and acceptance and abundant peace. Here is what is sacred, and here is what is deeply meaningful. Here too, is what is joyful, comforting and a sense of being home. Imagine feeling refreshed and rested in the arms of love itself, where you can truly be yourself. Imagine knowing that this is a place and a presence you can go to whenever you desire. Your home is here, carried in your own heart, waiting for you. All you need is to be still and remember Love is waiting.

> "Where can I go from your Spirit? Where can I flee from your Presence? If I go up to the heavens, you are there; if I make my bed in the depths, you are there. If I rise on the wings of the dawn, if I settle on the far side of the sea, even

there your hand will guide me, your right hand will hold me fast."

Psalm 139:7–10

Take a Moment to Listen:

Your true home, my child is with me, safe in my love and surrounded by my peace. This is your true inheritance. You were created for nothing less. Let my heart beat with yours as one, so you will know, without doubt, that I am always with you. My love is eternal and always waiting for you to come home to what is truly yours.

Guided Meditation

Go to your favorite quiet spot and once again sit down. Make yourself as comfortable as possible. Take a deep breath in and slowly exhale. Breathe in deeply once more and exhale slowly. As you take in deep breaths try to feel God's love all around you. Let yourself breathe in that love. Take as much time as you need. This is your sacred space.

As you sit with God, try and focus on the moments you felt most connected to him. Focus on what that felt like and what you were doing. Perhaps you were being quiet and still, not doing much of anything at all. If that was the case, can you remember that? Allow yourself to feel that deep and lovely connection once again. Sit with that feeling. Try and connect with God in a way that makes you feel safe and whole.

Try now to think about what it would mean for you to go out into the world with that lovely connection. How can you carry it with you and know that it is always there, waiting for you whenever you desire to feel it again.

Your Thoughts/Experience:

> *"Do not abandon yourself to despair. We are the Easter people and hallelujah is our song."*
>
> *John Paul II*

Life is often extremely difficult, and the heavy weight we regularly carry can easily drag us down. But we are not alone! There is always someone who travels with us and lights each step along the way of this rocky path.

It is often when we feel alone that despair can descend upon our hearts, as we look around terrified that we are sinking. If we can remember to change our perception just a little, we can remind ourselves that we are not carrying this weight alone. There is always help and guidance and healing that awaits our asking. Sometimes, even when we ask there appears to be a vast amount of silence. But perhaps we may be conflicted about what it is we want to hear. That conflict makes it difficult to have real clarity. It is not that God has abandoned us, but that we have our hand covered over our ears because we are not sure we really want to hear. We are so ambivalent about a particular outcome.

Perhaps also, we get way too far ahead of ourselves and ponder decisions we are far from being ready to make. But love lights the way in each step we take. Perhaps not ten steps ahead, but the one that is right in front of us. If we can just look for help where we are, we would probably be a lot less conflicted. Then we can take our hands away from our ears and listen with confidence and love. That is because love knows where we are emotionally, and what we need to know. Which is probably a lot less then what it is that we demand. Love lights each step and we are not alone. It's okay to ask for directions on the step we are standing on. That is a cause for joy.

> "The sun will no more be your light by day, nor will the brightness of the moon shine on you, for the Lord will be your everlasting light, and God will be your glory."
>
> Isaiah 60–19

Take a Moment to Listen:

Clarity is always present to you, and only awaits your joyful acceptance. You need not feel decisions are to be made alone in silent despair. Little child, love will forever light your way.

Guided Meditation:

Go to your favorite quiet spot and make yourself comfortable. Take a deep breath, and exhale slowly. Ask God to be with you as you slowly begin to relax. Try to feel God's love and peace all around you. Breathe it in. Feel it throughout your body.

Think about an issue that you would like guidance with. Ask God to help you now to have clarity. Is it an issue where you might be too far ahead of yourself? Think about that, if that is the case. Also try and be very honest with yourself. Are you conflicted about the outcome you would like to have? If that is so, then think about that. Be honest with yourself and with God about your mixed feelings and desires. Ask God to help you to sort your feelings out. If you are divided about what you want, then it is hard to move forward.

Let God help you to better understand your conflict. Are you conflicted because you are partly afraid? Then ask for help with that as well. Ask God to help you look at whatever fears might be holding you back from having clarity. Take as long as you need. There is no hurry. Sit with God and try to be open to what he may want you to know and understand.

Deborah J. Simmons-Roslak & Linda J. Orber

Your Thoughts/Experience:

> "I looked in temples, churches, and mosques, but I found the divine within my heart
>
> *Rumi*

Rituals are safe. Community rituals feel even safer and societal rituals carry with them the stamp of justified approval. No harm, no foul, consistent rituals are the cotton batting against bumps, rude shocks and bruising especially when wrapped around one's heart. Unfortunately, those same safe rituals can become an ideal hiding place.

Rituals present a conundrum. While the shared commonality of rituals weave a sense of comfortable surety around the lives of their constituents, they also become a justification or projection, or worse a reason for looking in all of the wrong places for all of the right things.

Searching for a connection to the divine is as time honored as humankind itself. We want to know that there is something, somewhere that intimately knows us, loves us and lends a guiding hand so to speak when we cannot see our way out of the fog.

The fear is that we are indeed alone in the universe like just so much carelessly occurring random matter. The twin to 'the alone in the universe' fear is the fear of unworthiness. Flip sides of the same coin, both fear based scenarios accomplish the same goal: keeping us away from a connection to the divine.

If our intent is to seek the divine, the pretense of seeking it only within the realm of either rituals and/or fear must be clearly understood. We are in the divine and the divine dwells within each and every one of us. The journey inward is as long or short, difficult or easy as we make it.

DEBORAH J. SIMMONS-ROSLAK & LINDA J. ORBER

> *"You will seek me and find me when you seek me with all your heart."*
>
> Jeremiah 29-13

Take a Moment to Listen:

Precious child, you are the beloved of heaven itself! Nothing could be withheld from you, as love by its very nature cannot withhold. The love that you seek, waits eagerly for your acceptance, for the love that you seek is already your own. It flows freely and willingly without end or limitation. How could such a bountiful love ever withhold itself from the beloved that it ever seeks in return?

Surrender the useless fears that serve as barriers to that which you seek. Come drink from Love's cup.

Guided Meditation:

Find a comfortable spot in which to sit. Close your eyes. Breathe in deeply. Exhale slowly and completely. Breathe in deeply again. Exhale slowly and completely. As you exhale, see yourself standing in front of the ocean. Smell the salt in the air as the waves roll rhythmically on to the shore spraying droplets against the sky. Breathe in again deeply. Exhale completely. Watch as the ocean tide slides slowly and surely back into itself, as it yet gathers itself to curl once again. Hear the sounds of the water crashing forward and lapping back gently.

Each wave though independent flows back into the ocean from where it gathers strength once more. We are like this. We are those waves as surely as the love of heaven is the ocean from where we gather strength. Breathe in deeply. As you exhale, listen to the sounds that fill you. Be at peace.

Your Thoughts/Experience:

> *"Let us not seek to satisfy our thirst for freedom by drinking from the cup of bitterness and hatred."*
>
> *Martin Luther King Jr.*

Hatred and bitterness is toxic to our souls. It clouds our judgment and dims our deepest light. From the well of this poison, we do not recognize our brother and sister, for we no longer recognize ourselves.

Our thinking, clouded by rage, neither sees nor hears other possibilities that could carry us along a far better path. It is here that we need help. It is here that we need a hand to lift us back to the light. In the light of just the smallest fragment of forgiveness we can open up to viewing a situation through the eyes of peace.

What possibilities are there, looking from such a kinder, gentler view? How can we move forward holding the hand of peace itself? These questions cannot be asked nor answered while holding tightly to the cup of bitterness. Indeed, hatred would preclude even remembrance of the hand of peace.

Our freedom is dependent upon the light of acceptance, forgiveness and truth. It grows in accord with the light that we allow to guide our every thought. There is power and unending strength in that guidance. There is wholeness, healing and peace.

> *"You have heard how it was said, you will love your neighbor and hate your enemy. But I say this to you, love your enemies and pray for those who persecute you; so that you will be children of your Father in heaven. Matthew 5:43-44*

Deborah J. Simmons-Roslak & Linda J. Orber

Take a Moment to Listen:

Hate and bitterness my child, are no treasure to store. Holding on to either is lonely and pain filled. It will not heal your heart, nor will it bring you the peace you so desperately seek.

In the midst of your rage—call me. I am already here. I will gently lift you as I have done so many times before. Here in this expansive light you will see more clearly. Here are other boundless possibilities that hate has clouded from your view.

Judgments made with love and in love do not cause pain my child. Instead love and forgiveness will always create hope. It is within that hope where your freedom lies. It is within that freedom where your peace is reborn once again.

Guided Meditation

There are moments when you feel uncomfortably alone. Perhaps no one understands what you are experiencing. Maybe you feel that no one really wants to listen. Maybe you have held on to negative perceptions for so long that it is impossible to feel the goodness and light alive and shining within you still. It is easy to completely forget that there is someone who is here and who wants to listen to your every need.

Close your eyes and take a deep breath. Let the breath go. Take another deep breath and exhale completely. In your mind's eye place yourself on a grassy hilltop. It's a quiet place. From here you can see a large oak tree. The leaves of the tree are swaying in the soft wind. There is a mother deer and her foal walking toward the brush. It's quiet and peaceful here, but you are never alone. God is here. He wants you to know that he is with you.

Tell God what you feel. If there are times you feel alone, let him know. Tell him everything you are thinking and feeling. When you are finished sharing, listen. Allow yourself to hear his answer. Allow yourself to feel his love for you.

Your Thoughts/Experience

> "I am poor and naked, but I am the chief of this nation. We do not want riches but we do want to train our children right. Riches would do us no good. We could not take them with us to the other world. We do not want riches. We want peace and love."
>
> Red Cloud, Oglala Lakota Sioux (1822–1909)

Imagine if all those who chased money instead, wanted to teach their children compassion. Imagine those same people wanting to teach a way of love, of peace and of kindness. So many live their lives filled with not only greed, but a deep emptiness that money can never satisfy. No matter how much money they acquire, it is never enough. It is a deep and endless cavern that can never be filled, because it is an emptiness that cannot be filled with what will not last. It is an emptiness that they never stop in stillness to try and understand.

It is just as easy for us to get caught up in the same way of thinking. We end up comparing ourselves to others and having a need to 'keep up'. We end up losing sight of the values that truly matter to us. We spend time chasing what we can't take with us, rather then what we will truly leave behind. We become so focused on the superficial and the ephemeral that we forget to listen to our own hearts.

If we can begin to listen to what we hear deep inside of us, we will remember that love is always what fills our hearts. It is love, kindness and compassion that warms our souls and brings us true joy. It is when we give to another in true freedom that we feel most happy. Love is a path waiting to be walked. Love is always inviting us to follow its light. It is a light that could never be extinguished, for love is eternal and it is what a child of God rightfully deserves, nothing less.

The superficial will come and go with the changing of the wind, but love is eternal and we were created to hold love in our hearts and share it with all those around us. It is in that sharing that we will find true and lasting joy.

> "Start children off on the way they should go, and even when they are old they will not turn from it."
>
> Proverbs 22:6

Take a Moment to Listen:

Love, compassion and kindness my child is your birthright. You desire nothing less. Life is filled with what is temporary, and that shall fade away in time, as it can never be eternal. Seek instead what your heart is asking, for that is where your joy is. Teach those around you of the love and peace that is theirs, for that is everlasting. You were created in and through love and love belongs to you. Allow yourself to dwell in love's light. Let that light shine as you walk through the world, for it is that light that will heal the hearts of others and what will truly bring you lasting joy.

Guided Meditation:

Find your favorite quiet spot and ask God to join you. Breathe in his love and his peace. Take some time as you let yourself feel God's presence. There is no rush. Take your time.

Think about what it is that you value. Think about what truly gives you joy. Let yourself remember a time that you felt really joyful and filled with love. Think about what you were doing and what it was that made you so happy. Let yourself remember that feeling of abundant joy.

Now think about the possibility that you might have moved away from doing or acting in a way that made you happy. If that's true what do you think happened? Did you get a little side tracked from what your heart was telling you? If that's true let yourself think about that. Ask God to help you to understand what happened.

Now think about what brings you true joy. How do you think you can have more of that? Sit with God and ask him to help you to find ways to answer what is in your heart. Let yourself truly listen and take your time. There is no rush. Let God help you to find more joy in your life.

Your Thoughts/Experience:

> "Grace is everywhere as an active orientation of all created reality toward God."
>
> Karl Rahner

Guideposts are needed, especially for those of us who are directionally challenged. The genius invention of the GPS system allows us to come and go at will with the confidence that we will arrive at our destination in a reasonable way. We rely upon navigation systems much as a household item in this day and age and are grateful for their existence. Navigation of a spiritual path however, can be confusing, confounding or simply troublesome. Where to begin? Who to turn to for advice? Is this even reasonable? It is at this point that navigation seems complicated and at times downright frightening.

What if however, our spiritual navigation system was a 'built in' feature, by virtue of being human? What if every breath we breathed sent us updated information from which we can know what decisions to make, which way to choose, or how to proceed. What if that navigation system was indeed our very link to our oneness, our wholeness and our road toward completion? What if?

> "There are different kinds of gifts, but the same Spirit distributes them. There are different kinds of service, but the same Lord. There are different kinds of working, but in all of them and in everyone it is the same God at work."
>
> Corinthians 4-6

Listen for a Moment

Just as the wind curls around every living thing, the rain drops its bounty on the thirsty everywhere and the same air is drawn into the bodies of all created, abundant heavenly grace bestows upon all the gifts of wholeness, of joy and of love.

Child—you could not ever be forgotten, or lost, as whom you are in truth is etched into the very fabric of heaven itself. Grace is freely given. Still your mind, let fear not take your holy inheritance from your hungry heart. Know that no fear is stronger then the love of heaven, no nightmare could erase the power of wholeness that is your birthright.

Accept what is your own by virtue of creation, take love's hand and know who you are in truth. Allow the grace of heaven to flow freely through you in every moment.

Guided Meditation

Find a comfortable place in which to sit. Relax into your space. Close your eyes. Inhale deeply and exhale completely. Sink deeper into your space. Inhale deeply again and exhale completely. Feel the air against your skin, your hands, your face, how it touches every part of you. Inhale deeply again and exhale completely.

Just as the air touches all of you so does the grace of God. Just as you can feel the air on your hands or on your face, so too there is nowhere that the grace of God is not. Within the grace of heaven is profound peace and surety. Within the grace of heaven is joy and gratitude for the being of all created.

Invite God to be with you in this moment. Become aware of the presence of grace surrounding you. Allow this grace to fill you as you inhale and exhale. Can you feel the presence of God with you in this moment?

Sit with the presence of God and the grace of heaven. Drink it in. This is your birthright and inheritance.

Your Thoughts/Experience

"All sins are attempts to fill voids"

Simone Weil

How often do we find ourselves gleefully skipping through a mall, or shopping arena, credit card in hand, ready and eager to spend hard earned money? The question is however, what is it we truly desire? Is it really those new boots, or is it something far more profound? It often feels as if something deep inside of us is missing, and those boots, this bracelet, or even that drink, will fill us with that special something we feel that we lack. We can't always put our finger on it, but it feels as if, deep down there is a need that we just can't seem to satisfy. So we tend to look outside of ourselves to find that special something to end the search. It might be we find it in clothing, or jewelry, or an expensive vacation. But once we have that item, or have taken that vacation, that feeling of emptiness seems to call to us once again. The satisfaction of that purchase doesn't seem to actually last for very long.

What if however, we began to look deep inside of ourselves and found something far more valuable? Imagine, if we realized, as we looked inside our own hearts, that we truly weren't alone. There is someone who loves us more than we can ever begin to understand. He not only wants to love us, but also wants us to share that love with those who cross our paths. What if each time we felt empty, we went to our source, and discovered that all of those outside purchases weren't necessary or even all that satisfying. That is because deep within our hearts is something so much more profound, and lovely and healing, then a pair of boots. Once we truly discover that, all the rest pales in comparison, for what can ever compare to absolute, eternal unconditional love? What can compare with a love that continually calls us to share in his exceptional and exquisite peace and profound and healing joy?

> "But store up for yourselves treasures in heaven, where are moths and vermin do not destroy, and where thieves do not break in and steal."
>
> Matt: 6:20

Take a Moment to Listen

Allow my love to fill your soul little child with all that I eternally offer you. What need is there for things that will never satisfy your lovely, tender heart? Do not look outward for desires that do not, nor cannot matter. Instead look within your own heart and you will find what it is that you truly treasure. My love is always yours, and that love is the deepest desire of your seemingly empty heart, for I have placed it there in your very creation. My eternal love will always be your treasure, and you my child are mine.

Guided Meditation

As you sit down in your favorite quiet spot, take a deep breath once again an close your eyes. Ask God to be with you as you begin to sense his presence all around that within you. Take as long as you need to feel his peace and his presence.

Think about the time you felt you wanted something that you didn't really need. Perhaps it might have been an item of clothing, or jewelry or something more. Do you remember what you wanted so badly and what that felt like? Think about that feeling for a while. Do you remember how excited you were in getting whatever this item was? Let yourself think about that for a while also. Now think about what you felt after having the item and some time passed. Did your joy with that piece of clothing, or jewelry or anything seem to genuinely last? Did you notice after some time that you felt a need for something else that would bring you happiness? What was that experience like? Let yourself be really honest.

Now think about the times when you felt God was truly with you. Think about when you felt his peace and his lasting presence. What was that like? How did you experience that? Is there a difference between the excitement of purchasing an item and the profound peace you felt with God? When you felt God was with you, did you feel a need for anything else, or did you feel whole and complete? If that is true let yourself ponder that experience, and feel God with you once again.

Your Thoughts/Experience

> "The weak can never forgive. Forgiveness is an attribute of the strong."
>
> Mahatma Ghandi

It can take courage, fortitude and tremendous strength to let go of old, tired grievances. It can seem so much easier to hold them tightly to our chest as if they were worthy of such an embrace. For some, any slight can bare witness to a sense of being victimized and we often proudly wear that hurtful crown.

Those who hold on to slights and collect hurts like a small treasure see the world as a very angry and hostile place. They expect the world to be both cruel and unforgiving and so their own grievances stay securely anchored to the bottom of their hearts.

It takes a great amount of compassion, generosity and understanding to forgive another's faults. For someone to do so, would mean that they can look inward and honestly try and understand another's pain and fear. Sometimes, they might even begin to see a similar trait within themselves as well. For those who can forgive another's fault, they also forgive that fault in themselves. For this, there needs to be both honesty and a sense of kindness not only towards another, but also towards and for themselves.

As we increase our understanding, compassion and forgiveness of those around us, we also do so for ourselves. In this way, we learn to be a little more kind with our own hearts, as we are with those around us therefore, those who learn to forgive begin to see a world reflected back that is a little more gentle, a little more caring, and a little more compassionate. The world becomes less hostile and more loving, and we begin to find a God that is far more loving then ever imagined.

DEBORAH J. SIMMONS-ROSLAK & LINDA J. ORBER

> *"And when you stand praying, if you hold anything against anyone, forgive them, so that your Father in heaven may forgive you your sins."*
>
> Mark 11:25

Take a Moment to Listen:

As you forgive, little child, so you will begin to see the world as a much more loving place, reflected back to you in complete gentleness. For here is a greater sense of peace and certainty. As you forgive, you will begin to watch the darkness slowly fade, as you perceive the world in kindness and tender peace. Take my hand and let me help you to let go of all the grievances that hold you back from the light of my joy for here is both your freedom and your peace.

Guided Meditation

Find your favorite spot and close your eyes. Gently relax and ask God to be with you. Take some time as you begin to think about any grievance you might be holding on to. Take your time as you think about this honestly. Think about how they might be affecting you, or preventing you from feeling more peaceful. Let yourself really think about how these grievances might be holding you back in some way. Ask God to help you with this.

Now think about what it would be like to be able to let your grievances and hurts go. Imagine how you might feel and how their absence might affect you differently. Again take your time, as you let yourself really ponder the absence of thoughts that were making you miserable. What do you think would be different in the way you might live, or in the way you perceive the world around you? Again take your time as you think about this. Do you think you feel more free and more peaceful? What do you imagine that to be like? As you begin to imagine this possibility, ask God to help you to let go of what is holding you back. Let yourself feel the peace that begins to fill the space that was previously occupied by old and tired grievances.

Now listen to anything God wants to say to you within your own heart. Again take your time and sit with him for a while. He wants to fill your heart with his peace and his joy. Let yourself feel that as you begin to let go of your hurts. Then sit with God, cradled in his love and in his peace.

Your Thoughts/Experience:

> *"To say that I am made in the image of God is to say that love is the reason for my existence for God is love. Love is my true identity. Selflessness is my true self. Love is my true character. Love is my name."*
>
> Thomas Merton

We often say that God is love, but find it extremely difficult to truly believe that idea. The very thought that we were created in love and for love, becomes difficult to comprehend, as we are not always loving ourselves. We imagine that God must tend to be as fickle and vacillating with his emotions as we are. We are pretty certain, that when we are filled with fear, and act accordingly, God must be disgusted with us. This is because we are so easily disgusted with ourselves.

There are moments however, when love does take hold of our hearts, and we delight in the world around us. We see through the eyes of grace, compassion and gentleness. In those moments that we are kind to others, we are also kind to ourselves, and feel connected to God who is eternally loving and kind. What gets in our way is our own selves. We hold a grudge in our heart and expect God to do the same. We forget that love doesn't change. It is we who trip over our own vacillating emotions. We expect God, to think and behave as we do, and it's hard to comprehend that love itself is perpetual and eternal.

Therefore, the kinder we become to others, the kinder we become to ourselves. In that kindness we truly begin to see God far more clearly as wholly and completely gentle and loving. We were created in love, by love itself. As we become a little gentler moving in and through the world, we will come to understand that love is indeed who we are and who our creator is and always was.

> "No one has ever seen God; but if we love one another, God lives in us and His love is made complete in us."
>
> *John 4:12*

Take a Moment to Listen:

You were, my child, created in love and by love. Your heart was created for nothing less. Do not let yourself be fooled by fleeting emotions that tend to frighten you in the darkness. Love is your inheritance and gentleness is your eternal and unwavering guide. The more loving your heart becomes, the more you will know the truth of your own lovely spirit. Open your heart to my kindness, love and gentleness and you will remember the love that you truly are.

Guided Meditation

Go to your favorite quiet space where you can truly relax and feel at peace. Ask God to be with you. Gently settle in to his love and his peace. Let yourself feel wrapped in his tenderness.

Allow yourself to think about when you might have felt most disconnected to God. What happened, and what do you think about when you might have felt most disconnected to God. What happened, and what do you think you were feeling? Was your heart closed off for some reason? If that is true, what happened? Think about that and what that felt like.

Now, think about when you felt most connected to God. Take your time as you really think about that. What was that like and what were you feeling? Do you recall your heart being more open to those around you? Let yourself think about that experience. In those moments, did you also feel a little more loved and connected to God? Let yourself stay with those thoughts and that experience for a while.

What do you think helped you to open your heart? Ask God to help you to understand that experience. Perhaps you would like to have those experiences more often. Ask God to help you. What do you think you need to do to have a more open heart?

Now sit with God for a while and talk to him about anything you discovered. Then, listen with your heart to anything you think he wants to let you know. Take your time and sit with God in his love and in his peace.

Your Thoughts/Experience:

"No one can help the fish to find the ocean."

Anthony DeMello

Looking for God in and through marvelous signs and wonders can seem like a spiritual path. The bigger those signs and wonders the better we feel about our 'pathway home'. We can breathlessly exclaim to have experienced a this or a that, or have seen the 'vision of the century', which of course will be responded to by someone else's marvelous signs and wonders. It's as if God must continually prove existence in a human conceived outstanding, amazing story of the year sort of way. While we are entrenched in playing the ego-based game of who has the 'bigger god story', it will not occur to us to look inward.

Perhaps, God is in the very silence of our own being. Yet we hardly ever look there. We love talking about the wonders of nature and outer space and all manner of spectacular phenomenon. We love to look at nature's magnificent trees and that wondrous star, shining in the silky black night. We point to it as a lovely reflection of God's abundant and amazing creation, but we often fail to look inside our own hearts and minds as a resting place for God's very presence.

When we are very quiet and can stop all the noxious noises around us—we can sense God's omnipresence within us. We can feel his eternal peace. We know in those moments, without a wavering doubt, that he is indeed here, deep inside our hearts. We can hear him whisper our name with delight.

Perhaps we can begin to learn that we don't need to find God outside of ourselves anymore than a fish would need to find the ocean. The ocean surrounds and envelops that fish, just as God wraps his benevolent arms around us. There is nowhere the fish can swim where there is no ocean. There is nowhere we can go without God, for God rests forever in the very center of our own souls. Once we recognize that, then your inner space will be just as amazing as the stars.

> *"What agreement is there between the temple of God and idols? For we are the temple of the living God. As God has said; I will live with them and walk among them, and I will be their God, and they will be my people."*
>
> 2 Corinthians 6:16

Take a Moment to Listen:

My precious child, I am always with you since your very creation and indeed I could never leave my own joy. My heart rests with yours in every moment, as I bring you inspiration, strength and continual peace. My love will heal your heart and lift your soul when you are in need of comfort and your weary soul longs to be healed. Love asks nothing and gives everything in complete willingness and joy. Know my child that my very heart is your inheritance and I delight in your being.

Guided Meditation:

When you find your most comfortable space, sit down and let your body relax. Feel that relaxation rom the top of your head to the bottom of your feet. Try and relax every part of you. Now invite God to be with you. Take a deep breath and try and feel his presence with you, and within you. Try and rest in his presence and peace. Take as much time as you need.

Think about the moments that you were in awe of nature. Can you remember a particular moment when you felt a deep sense of both awe and peace as you looked at something that astounded you? Try and think about that moment and what you were feeling and what that was like. Now think about the moments that you felt God was with you. Do you remember a moment in time that you could feel that presence with you and knew without a doubt that God was there? Try to think about that for a while and what that experience was like. Take your time with it. Can you allow yourself to feel that again, knowing he is here with you now? What is that experience like? Can you call on him now to experience his presence and peace? Let yourself know that you can call on him and ask for his help at any moment in your life. What does that feel like, knowing that he is always there resting eternally in your own heart?

Your Thoughts/Experience:

> "Re-examine all you have been told. Dismiss what insults your soul."
>
> *Walt Whitman*

It is not uncommon to have grown up within a toxic environment where the poison spouted every day within our earshot was soaked up to be used against ourselves at some future date and time. Those voices and that poison reverberate like a cacophony of horrendous clanging that does not leave our exhausted minds. It often becomes our wear mantra: you aren't, you can't, you won't. Many never question these hideous, toxic messages.

Imagine if we began to actually question that harmful drumbeat inside our minds. What if we allowed ourselves to recognize, that those harsh and awful indictments were not worthy of a child of God? If God created us in love and with love, it is only the voices of fear that hold us hostage. It is the voices of fear that scream in the darkness falsely accusing us of being unworthy. What if we decided not to listen?

If we could instead listen with the heart of love, even for a moment, we would understand that there is a far more beautiful and sacred music calling to us. It is that lovely and beautiful music that God wants us to hear. The gentle sounds of wholeness softly call us to become who we in truth are. We were meant to love and to be loved and that is what should be etched upon our lovely souls. All the other noise is nothing that matters.

Love completely wraps its arms around us and whispers our name. Love calls to us that we were created in love and deserve nothing less. We are asked to allow ourselves to be loved and to share that love in a circle of joy. Love is what created us, and we fully and completely belong to love. All the darkened noise will drift away in the glorious sound of love's sacred call to our wear hearts.

> "See what great love the Father has lavished on us, that we should be called children of God! And that is what we are! The reason the world does not know us is that it did not know him."
>
> 1 John 3:1

Take a Moment to Listen:

You, my child, are absolutely cherished and loved, far beyond what you can now comprehend. I wrap my arms around your heart, and watch your every step in tenderness and delight. Do not listen to the sounds of fear, for they are nothing. You are cherished and held and loved in every moment. Love is who you are and I delight in your very being. Let your heart join with mine and listen as I whisper your name in joy. You are my cherished child whom I completely and eternally love.

Guided Meditation:

Find your favorite quiet spot and sit down. Take a deep breath and relax. Ask God to be with you. Stop for a while and quietly feel God's love surrounding you and filling your heart with peace.

Think about the negative thoughts that you often tell yourself. Really think about how these negative thoughts and ideas influence you. Take your time with this and ask God to help you as you look at this together. Have these thoughts stopped you from moving forward or from feeling positive about yourself? When do you let yourself acknowledge them? Are they something that you heard in childhood? Let yourself understand that these indictments are often from people who are filled with fear them selves.

Now ask God to help you hear his call to you. Let yourself listen to him tell you how much he treasures you and loves you. Allow yourself to hear that you are his child and his love for you is eternal and nothing will change that. Let yourself listen with an open and deserving heart. Sit with God for as long as you need to and listen to everything he wants to tell you. Let yourself know how loved you truly are. Wrap yourself in his love and his peace. Soak in that love and take that love with you out into the world. You are loved and cherished. You belong to him and he loves you eternally.

Your Thoughts/Experience:

"You don't have a soul. You are a soul. You have a body."

C.S. Lewis

Identifying ourselves as who we know ourselves to be is commonplace. All sorts of identification are needed. Drivers licenses, social security cards, green cards, visas, passports all guarantee that the face and the number match the body in possession of the paperwork. Simple. Yet not. Identifying ourselves with our bodies leads to a great preoccupation with the state of that body. There are constant communications and notices of every minute change in the condition of that body, and remedies to correct any unpleasant condition that body may encounter. The world is full of bodies. Yes?

The world rotates around the physical and the superficial. Here is a world filled with a preoccupation of having the most sought after items to adorn or enhance a body, the best of health and care products to protect that same body. Bodies are something we can see. Bodies make it easier for us to identify friend or foe. We can hang a hat on one, wear shoes on one, laugh or growl with one. Bodies seem to revel in competition with other bodies. There are winning bodies and non-winning bodies. There's no disputing that we have a physical self, but total identification with that physical self denies the fullness of our being human.

If the nonphysical is summarily dismissed however, so too is the dismissal of a deeper perception, an inner life, a soul and a spirit. Dismissal or non-recognition of who we are in completion, rejects the gentleness of spirit and the wisdom of the soul. The awareness of our complete being is the awareness of a shared grace, a connection to all of creation through the gift of divine love. The soul has a physical body, one in which to affect a physical world with healing, peace and the gentleness of divine spirit.

> *"Indeed, while following the way of Your judgments, O LORD, We have waited for You eagerly; Your name, even Your memory, is the desire of our souls."*
>
> Isaiah 26:8

Take a Moment to Listen

Beautiful child, in the very richness of your creation, you were given all the most lovely and everlasting gifts. Here, was a tender and gentle heart, meant for everlasting love. Here was a grace that follows you from this very moment into all of eternity. What need then is there of superficial trappings? The light in your soul shines brighter than any object ever could. Your joy is your acceptance of that love, along with your joyful sharing. Your soul was given love, light and beauty. Let that shine through all the darkness of the world. For here is your truest joy, and the song your heart yearns to eternally sing.

Guided Meditation

Sit down in your favorite quiet space. Take a deep breath in and relax your entire body. Ask God to join you, as you breathe in his love and his peace. Think about how often you identify with your body. How often do you find yourself preoccupied with the state of your body, or the state of other bodies. If bodies matter, how often do you find yourself competing with other bodies?

Take another deep breath, and begin to think about how different your life would be if you perceived yourself as a soul. Imagine if instead of the state of your body being crucial, the light and love inside your heart mattered more.

Ask God to help you recognize and share the gifts that are already inside your heart. Sit with God as you listen to anything he wants you to know. Allow yourself to rest in his peace. Take as long as you need as you sit in this quiet and gentle space. Then take that love into the world.

Your Thoughts/Experience

> "To pray is to let God into our lives. He knocks and seeks admittance, not only in the solemn hours of secret prayer. He knocks in the midst of your daily work, your daily struggles, your daily grind. This is when you need Him most."
>
> Ole Hallsby

Minute by minute, hour by hour we skid through our complicated lives, concerned, but not always focused on our next important step. Absent-mindedly completing one task, so we can quickly finish and move on to the next, there remains an inner emptiness when the noise of the day finally ceases. There is a quiet yearning that wishes we had better insight, clearer guidance in our decisions and more comfort in our uneventful chores. We often feel alone.

Rarely do we notice in the ebb and flow of our lives that we are not alone. There is a gentle whisper of our name deep within the very center of our being. Here, there is calmness, a sense of certainty and gentle peace waiting for us with open arms. Slow down and listen, for in this sacred moment in the center of our lives, we can hear him call our name. In the midst of our decisions, and all the mundane and complicated activity there is absolute gentleness and perfect peace. Here, in this moment of calm, are the answers we are seeking, for here is the answer itself.

In this presence, loneliness and boredom quietly dissipate, as love fills even the most frightened heart. God is perpetually calling, and his guidance and friendship are endlessly waiting for our acceptance. All we must do is slow down and be still for just a moment. That is all it takes. In that very moment we are certain of love's presence, as it fills our hearts. We can once again feel the peace we have been so longing for. He will call to us until we hear him. Divine love is and always was tucked inside our hearts.

> *"I will give you hidden treasures, riches stored in secret places, so that you may know that I am the LORD, the God of Israel, who summons you by name."*
>
> Isaiah 45:3

Take a Moment to Listen

I have gently knocked upon the center of your tender heart since the dawning of your creation. You are mine, and I call you by name. If you would listen for just a moment in quiet stillness, you would hear me. I would be your companion and your comfort in all that you do.

I will whisper to you over again, until you listen, for my love waits only to heal your tired and frightened heart. Let me be all that you need, and I will give you all that I am.

Guided Meditation

Relax in your favorite space and try and slow down. Take a deep breath and feel God's love with you. Let yourself think about how busy you have been and what that business feels like. Are you anxious, stressed or uncertain? Think about times that you may have felt lonely or especially worried. Maybe there were times when you felt bored. Let yourself really think about that for a little while.

During any of those moments did you seek God's help, guidance, or companionship? If not, ask yourself why. What do you think might have stopped you from seeking his help or healing? Take your time as you think about this. You can ask God to help you to understand your reluctance in a clearer way. Let him help you to understand what stopped you from feeling his love, guidance, or his presence. Take as long as you need.

Now think about the present moments in your life. Would you like more of his guidance, comfort or healing? Can you allow yourself to ask for that as you sit with him. Let him know what it is you are seeking. Ask for his help. Sit with God for as long as you need to and listen for anything he wants to tell you. Let yourself feel safe in his love and his peace. Try and remember as you go about your everyday life that love is never absent from your heart.

Your Thoughts/Experience

> *"The power of God is with you at all times; through the activities of mind, senses, breathing, and emotions; it is constantly doing all the work using you as a mere instrument."*
>
> Bhagavad Gita

When love flows through us, there is an infinite power that is so much greater than our little selves. We almost feel tiny in comparison. We can feel that sense and know that we are connected to something so much more than who we believe we are. In those moments of astonishing grace, we speak in harmony with the Voice of Love and move in the direction love guides us. We are open to its quiet peace and abundant joy and unlimited power that is difficult to fathom. We don't need to fear our next step. In those moments, we absolutely know that we are guided by a power far greater than ourselves. We can feel it with us and within our very being.

Love lies in the hearts of every child of God and constantly whispers its compassionate guidance. For those who are open to love's own whispers, they move through life, acting, speaking and even breathing love's own song. It is a grace that is shared in the movements of those that have opened their hearts to love's desires. It is a grace that everyone is invited to share. Love leaves out no one, as love is always inclusive. God's love desires to embrace every child in love, comfort, tenderness and indeed joy. Love asks to share abundantly. All we need to do is open our own hearts and allow love to move through us as the mighty force that it is. Love only desires an open heart. If we can open the heart that God has given to us, he will guide us in everything we do. Love will shine as a light for those around us and we will experience the joy God desires we have.

> "Don't you know that you yourselves are God's temple and that God's Spirit dwells in your midst."
>
> Corinthians 3:16

Take a Moment to Listen

There is never a moment in time I do not look upon my beloved child with anything but complete and total love. I hold you in the center of my heart, and wrap my arms around yours, calming your fears and giving peace to your anxious soul. I am there with you, through all that you do, knowing what you need for your heart to be healed. Turn to me whenever you are fearful. Turn to me whenever you have suffered a fall. I am here to lift you up and remind you of my eternal love for you and how much I treasure your heart.

Guided Meditation

Find a quiet spot and sit down. Try and allow yourself to become as relaxed as possible. Invite God to be with you. Take your time and feel his presence all around and within you. Just sit with him for a while and breathe in his peace.

Think about a time when you truly feel that God was with you. Can you remember that experience? What did it feel like? Did you feel his guidance in something you were doing? Did you experience his love flowing through you in either your words or your actions? Try to remember what that experience felt like and sit with that for a while. Remember how connected you felt to God and how much more connected you felt to the person or people you were with.

Perhaps after thinking about it, you would like to experience that more often. How do you imagine that can happen? Let yourself really think about that. Talk to God about your desire. Ask him to help you to feel more open to his love, his peace and his presence.

Share with God how you feel about being more open to his love. Then listen. Try and listen to anything you think God wants to impart to you. Sit with him for as long as you feel a need. Soak in his love and his gentleness. Tell him anything that is on your mind about this or anything else you want him to know. Make this a time to share with him and also to listen. Open your heart and allow yourself to welcome him there.

Your Thoughts/Experience

"Pain is never permanent."

Teresa of Avila

In the midst of a crisis, it is usually almost impossible to see beyond what we feel emotionally. We are swimming for our lives, it feels like, and trying desperately to keep our heads above water. For many of us this sense of continual panic, dread, and misery appear to have no for seeable end. We often forget that things do change, and that whatever pain we are in now, might abate over a period of time. When we are sad, or lonely, or even feeling a deep sense of loss, we lose the awareness that those feelings as awful as they are, might dissipate in time. We feel stuck in whatever miserable, emotional state we are in and it becomes hard to find an exit sign.

However, in those moments, we can try to recall that our thoughts are constantly changing, much like the shapes of clouds on a clearer morning. What we thought at one moment might be reshaped in another moment. So our thoughts change, and so do our emotions along with them. None of this is permanent because as awful as it feels now, none of this is eternal. What is eternal and safe is tucked deep inside our hearts and that will not change. God's love is perpetual, eternal and wholly never ending. It is also immutable, as love cannot change what it, in fact is. If we can try and remember in this world of turmoil and turbulence, that thoughts and emotions will eventually change, and what we see now is temporary. God's love will last now and forever, as it was always meant to. We are created for that love and nothing else is truly worthy of a lovely child of God.

Love, God

"Give thanks to the Lord, for he is good. His love endures forever."

Psalm 136-1

Take a Moment to Listen

All the love that is tucked inside your heart is eternal little child. You were created for nothing less. Your fear and your pain will come and go- much like a dese fog that rolls in and will disappear in nature's light. So too, will my holy light shine away your darkened fears and you will know once again, the peace and the joy that is forever yours. Hold on to my hand and let me guide you through the dim and unclear fog. I will take you where you need to go in safety and in peace. Know that I am with you.

Guided Meditation

Sit down and relax your whole entire body. Inch by inch breathe in relaxation and exhale concern. After a few minutes try to feel God's presence around you and within you. Think about a time that you felt upset, troubled or particularly anxious. Can you recall that experience and remember what it was like? Do you remember how your feelings might have changed over time? Can you try and recall what began to happen that helped you to begin to feel differently? Was there anything in particular that helped you to feel less stressed? Let yourself think about that for a while. Was there anything in the way you understood the situation that might have changed? What was that? Again, let yourself think about that.

Is there anything that you are currently stressed or upset about? Take your time as you allow yourself to think about that. Ask God to help you to understand the situation in a different way. Sit quietly with God and let him heal your fear and your stress. Try and listen to anything you think he wants you to know or understand. Let him help you to see this current situation from a different point of view. Take your time with this and you allow

God to help heal your concern and your stress. Then sit with God wrapped in his love and his peace for as long as you need to. When you are ready to go out again into the world take that sense of love and peace with you.

Your Thoughts/Experience

"The poison of selfishness destroys the world."

Catherine of Sienna

Many of us look around at a world filled with indifference. We watch people walk by the homeless, the hungry and those in need. We watch as many look down upon those who don't have a shiny this or that as somehow inferior. They often look the other way at those who suffer mentally, physically and emotionally. They not only forget that this is our brother or sister, but they see a stranger they want nothing to do with—as if they would catch another's suffering.

Perhaps we cannot eradicate selfishness from those around us, but we can certainly become more aware of when we begin to recognize it in ourselves. What would it take to be a little kinder and little less indifferent? How can we ourselves show more kindness to those we meet? In spite of the indifference of many in the world, we can become aware of when we begin to behave in an indifferent manner, rather than a light of compassion and care.

If we can begin to become truly aware of our own behavior, we will begin allowing a space for love to enter. It is in our own awareness that we allow a quiet space of both love and light. Each time we notice our own failings, love is free to take hold of our hearts once again. It is not that we necessarily have to do anything in particular. However, if we can open ourselves up to love's light, that very light will guide us in our actions and in our words. What we most need to do is to get our own indifference out of the way. Love is already at work in our deepest heart. We need only let it be and open ourselves to its call.

Deborah J. Simmons-Roslak & Linda J. Orber

> "A new command I give you: Love one another. As I have loved you, so you must love one another."
>
> John 13:34

Take a Moment to Listen

Love is all-inclusive and asks for nothing. It desires nothing but only to give. When you have made space in your heart for love to abide, love itself will lead you. You need not worry what you need to say or do. Love will always lead you safely in every situation. Love seeks always to include and to give all that it holds. It seeks to bestow peace and eternal joy to everyone, leaving no child of God out of the infinite circle. Open your heart and let love lead you child. In those moments love will rush in and fill every space with nothing less than itself. In those moments you will be filled with Me as you recognize that love is eternally with you.

Guided Meditation

Find a quiet spot to sit and relax. Close your eyes and let yourself feel the love and peace of God all around you. Breathe it in and feel it filling your heart. Take your time allowing God's love to completely fill you.

Think about the people that you have met lately. Think about your interactions with them. Have you noticed at times a sense of indifference to someone's suffering? Let yourself know those answers honestly. Whatever you were thinking and feeling, share that with God. You are surrounded by his love and acceptance.

Ask God to help you to understand what happened when you were feeling indifferent. Do you think you were upset, or perhaps afraid? Ask God to help you understand that within your own heart. It's perfectly alright. God wants to help you understand. If you were upset or afraid ask him to help you with those feelings. Take as long as you need. Listen to anything God wants to say to you. You are safe and accepted completely. Sit with God as long as you need. Ask him to heal whatever is causing your fear, discomfort or indifference. Then sit with God and let him heal your heart.

Your Thoughts/Experience

> "The bible tells us to love our neighbors, and also love our enemies; probably because generally they are the same people."
>
> G.K. Chesterton

How easy it is to realize that someone we deeply and dearly love can, at times, get on our very last nerve. One moment we look at them with joy, gentleness and a deep admiration. It's not too long before that same person fills us with resentment, frustration and irritation. We can feel anger rising from the bottom of our toes flowing to the top of our heads. We are moment to moment filled with a multitude of different emotions.

But, perhaps what keeps us 'sane', is our ability to gently forgive. It is in forgiveness that we can love those that hate us and love those we previously hated just a short while ago. It is in those moments of forgiveness that we open ourselves up to a compassion and tenderness that is greater than our own. We then can look at those with whom we feel irritation and see them with a more meaningful vision. In those moments we can see with God's compassion.

We can then look at another and begin to comprehend that whatever irritable action they are engaged in might be difficult and upsetting for them as well. We are all filled with fear at times, and then we begin operating according to our perceived frightened thoughts.

Since it is often fear that drives us, it is in those moments that we most need comfort and a sense of reassurance. When our hearts are open to forgiveness, we open to God's love. We begin to perceive in a far different and understanding light. We then become a voice for reason and kindness. We also become a voice for healing, comfort and for peace. Whatever emotions flow through us, we can be assured that God's love and guidance is with us, if we can open our hearts to hear his call to forgive. Love then will light the way for us and we will begin to see our enemies with a sense of understand, compassion and love.

> "And when you stand praying, if you hold anything against anyone, forgive them, so that your Father in heaven may forgive you your sins."
>
> Mark 11:25

Take a Moment to Listen:

My precious child, open your heart to my call and let my love and light guide you. Forgive your brothers and sisters as you long to be forgiven. Deep in each heart is a desire for comfort and kindness from the frightening thoughts that often terrify. When you are uncertain, ask me to help you to see more clearly. I will open your heart to the call of forgiveness and the comfort of peace. Then, share that peace with those that so deeply need healing, for it will heal your heart as well.

Guided Meditation

Go to a place you feel most comfortable and sit. Relax. Take a deep breath as you close your eyes. Invite God to be with you. Sit for a moment wrapped in God's presence and his peace.

Allow yourself to wonder if there is anyone with whom you are angry, irritated, or frustrated with. Let yourself think about them and what it is that is making you angry or upset. Let yourself feel whatever feelings you are having about them. Now ask God to help you to see them with the eyes of forgiveness. Ask him to help you to understand what you might not know, or what you might not understand. Sit with him for awhile and ask him to help you to be more understanding. Take your time with this. If something is bothering you about them, ask God to help you see with his compassion. Listen to anything you think God may be trying to tell you—again there is no rush.

Does this help you to see this person in a clearer more compassionate way? How might that change your interactions with them? Ask God what you can do to help bring more clarity and peace into the situation. Then sit with God, surrounded by his love, peace and gentleness.

Your Thoughts/Experience

> "The best and the most beautiful things in this world cannot be seen or even heard, but must be felt with the heart."
>
> *Helen Keller*

In a world filled with stimulation and excitement, we are usually searching for our next adrenalin rush. There are visions of sparkling jewelry a closet of fabulous clothes, or a vacation with a view that takes our very breath away. After scoring a victory in any of these exciting categories, we are filled with great anticipation over our next incredible treasure. The world, it seems, is filled with a paragon of all manner of wonderful prizes and adventures to collect. Losing ourselves in quest after quest, to find the next stimulating find or experience, usually leads us to crave for more. There is always another fabulous, sought after item, or adventure. The hunt never ends—as the perfect find is just over the horizon.

Deep inside the heart, in a much more profound and lovely place, is a quiet joy that increases as the treasure that is inside of us is happily given away. There is no need for accumulated items or adventurous tales. Here, the joy is in sharing what is dearly held. In this place, joy is felt not with stimulation, or excitement, but with a lasting sense of quiet peace. The heart is open and desires to generously give all that it contains. Here is a quiet and joyful beauty that is held and shared in the deepest part of a loving heart. Here is a lasting peace that surpasses all of the pleasures in our line of vision, for something far more profound. In this lovely and lasting place the heart smiles at the love recognized in others. There is joy in the gentleness of life. Here is a place that brings rest to a weary soul and comforts the hearts of those who are hurting. In this place love is always the answer, and all the stimulation and excitement come to rest at last in loves own embrace.

> "As water reflects the face, so one's life reflects the heart."
>
> Proverbs 27:19

Take a Moment to Listen

As you go about your life sweet child, do so with an open and loving heart. Share all that your heart contains, and joyfully smile in delight at this delicate and lovely treasure. Here is a quiet peace and happiness that is always your truest joy. Join with me in giving all that truly matters, for here is the treasure your heart has sought all along. Tucked deep inside your heart is a treasure far greater then the ones the world offers you, for this lasting treasure that never empties or disappears. It is always replenished as it is given away. Here is the home of love itself and in this place is all that your heart has ever truly desired and all that will bring you peace.

Guided Meditation

Once again go to your favorite quiet spot, where you can relax and feel more at peace. Ask God to join you and take your time as you allow yourself to feel his presence.

Think about all the times you have felt very excited and stimulated as you felt a need to have certain items or a need to go to a certain place, or have a certain adventure. Think about what that felt like and the excitement of that need. Did you notice after you acquired the object or arrived at a particular place, it left you feeling a bit let down? If so, what was that like? Did you feel a need after some time, to acquire another item or have another adventure? Have you noticed that perhaps there is always a need to have something, or go somewhere? Take your time thinking about that.

Now think about the moments in your life, where your heart truly smiled in the sharing of love around you. Can you let yourself think about those moments and how different they felt? What was it like to just share joy and love rather than feel a need for something? What is the difference in your lasting happiness? Take your time as you really think about he difference in tone and feeling inside your heart. Would you like your joy and your peace to last longer? Can you ask God to help you to find ways to share the love and joy in your heart, rather than a constant need to find stimulation? Sit with God as you understand all that he has to tell you.

Your Thoughts/Experience

> "By means of all created things without exception, the divine assails us, penetrates us and molds us. We imagined it as distant and inaccessible when in fact we live steeped in its burning layers."
>
> Pierre Teilhard de Chardin

Individuality is held up as *the jewel* in the crown of human actualization. While prizing an individual's artistic, musical or intellectual gifts as they share those gifts with the world at large connects us to the individual through an extraordinary talent not self-given, it also merges us with deeper aspects of that individual. For here is shared beauty, symmetry, elegance in something so finely and artistically mastered. Their shared talent touches our hearts and captures our souls as we open our minds to something new. Here deep within each soul is a sacred beauty that at times seems hidden, but when opened and shared, brings joy to every heart that experiences its loveliness. Individuality however, can at times be used as a weapon to divide, categorize and toss aside.

Deep within every part of creation is the divine, which calls us to open to the wonder of all that has been hidden within our own hearts. When we let go of our fears and dare to look, we find a treasure of all the joy and loveliness that was given to us in our own creation. We open our hearts to the beauty of divine love that has always rested here. As we share that sacred gift, we feel a profound joy—for this was a gift that we were given to share in grace and humility. The divine calls to us, molds us, and is as accessible as our own hearts, for love is forever nestled deep within our souls and yearns only to be extended.

> "I will rise then and go about the city; in the streets and crossings I will seek Him whom my heart loves."
>
> Song of Solomon 3:2

Take a Moment to Listen

In all places and ways I am with you. You only need to make the slightest turn to see that I am here. Holy child, it is but for the asking that the love of all creation would fill you. It is but for the asking that the joy of our love flow through you and extend its own invitation in peace to all you meet.

Guided Meditation

We often choose fear instead of peace and resentment, instead of kindness. We often choose in ways that bring us more pain and often leaving us feeling alone and deprived. Find a quiet place and sit. Take a deep breath exhale completely. Invite God to be with you as you breathe in his love and surround yourself with his peace.

Think about the choices you make in a day. How many times have you chosen fear, or resentment without even realizing? How often do you react to something without taking a moment to take a step back in peace or understanding? Give yourself some space to think about this. What do you imagine it would like to realize you were reacting in fear, and then ask for God's help? How do you imagine that would change the way you work, live and move about in the world? Let yourself imagine what that would be like.

Then ask God to help you to be more aware of his presence in your life. Listen quietly to anything you think God wants to tell you. Sit with him in that peace.

Your Thoughts/Experience:

> *"Unless you are willing to do the ridiculous, God will not do the miraculous. When you have God, you don't have to know everything about it; you just do it."*
>
> *Mother Angelica*

In the stillness of our hearts, there is often a quiet sense of something we are asked to do. We don't quite understand it. Perhaps it's a bit out of our usual character, maybe out of our comfort zone as well, but it softly calls to us—like a familiar song we have somehow forgotten. Perhaps it calls us to help another, or reach out in compassion, or listen without judgment. It is often a gentle nudging, that pulls on our hearts and reminds us of love living deep within who we really are.

Sometimes we ignore the nudge as we dive into welcomed stimulating activity. We kick a lot of dust up, dulling the sound. But when we are still and alone, it continues to quietly haunt us. Often we resist doing what is asked, as we don't have it all figured out. After all, understanding it all is key to being successful. Yet the song plays in our hearts, as the melody rises deep inside. Perhaps not having it all figured out is all right. Maybe we begin with a small melodic note, just a tiny movement, like a kind word, a call to a friend, or an offer to assist. Not knowing where it will lead seems frightening, as we stick our foot in some commitment we don't quite understand. Yet, we know this matters, as the song continues to play in our soul.

There is something to be done, and we have been asked to do it. We know God has asked us, as we feel the pull in our heart, much like the waves feel the pull of the moon. If we can take a step forward in this small act, trusting his grace, perhaps we need not understand at all. Love is in charge and perhaps that is all we need to know.

> *"In God, whose word I praise—in God I trust and am not afraid. What can mere mortals do to me?"*
>
> Psalm 56:4

Take a Moment to Listen

My heart calls to yours my child, in joyous song and lovely melody. Love will call to the depth of your heart until, at last, you answer. You were created in love and love is who you are. My love is to be shared and you are always called to share it. There is no need for complete understanding, as I will guide your heart in all you do. There is only a need to respond to love's gracious call. I will sing you songs of love with melodies of joy that are always meant to be shared, until at last you hear.

Guided Meditation

Find a space to sit and relax. Take a deep breath and ask God to be with you. Take some time to feel yourself surrounded by God's love and peace.

Have you had an experience where you have been asked to reach out to another in some way? What was that experience like? What did you feel, as you somehow understood God was asking something of you that perhaps you weren't sure of. Take sometime to think about this experience, and perhaps the pull you felt to reach out. What was that experience like? What was it that you did, and how did it help another?

Now think about what it was like to know you have helped someone in some way? How did you feel about having reached out? Was it a feeling that stuck with you, even after the experience was over? What was it like to find a way to be loving that was a little unexpected?

Take some time as you explore whether there is something God wants you to do now? Has there been something God wants you to do now? Has there been something you have been thinking or wanting to do that is hard to shake off? Can you sit with God and ask about that? Try to let yourself listen to anything you think God wants you to know or understand about this. Take your time. Sit with God for as long as you need to as you allow yourself experience his love and his guidance.

Your Thoughts/Experience

> "There is no greater lifestyle and no greater happiness than that of having a continual conversation with God."
>
> Brother Lawrence

Love hears us. In the rushed activity of the day straight through to dusk, and then into the silky darkness of night—love listens. There is no moment where help cannot be asked for or joy cannot be shared. Love hears, but guides, comforts and heals our fearful thoughts and unsettled hearts. Love listens, with outstretched hands to heal our hurts and guide our faltering steps.

We often hold ourselves back, ignoring love's presence as we try alone to figure out our next move. We forget there is a hand on our shoulder leading us along each rocky path and uncertain step. If we still ourselves and remember love's presence, we would know in that moment we weren't alone. Guided by wisdom far beyond our own, we would quietly listen to Love's intervening response and then rest in the certainty that love listens with compassion and tenderness.

Imagine before asking anyone else to help us with a decision, we asked a far wiser friend who knows our hearts and understands life's outcomes. What would it mean to feel help lies deep within our own hearts, merely waiting to be asked? Love only desires to heal, share and comfort our fears and uncertainties. There is nothing we cannot share with the one who loves us most and understands our own heart's desire. We need only remember love's presence within us and all that love wants to impart.

We often seek to find an answer in the comfort of another, yet here is the answer we have been seeking that has never left us, nor ever would. All we need do is turn our focus just a little and open our hearts just enough, for love will come rushing in to respond to our smallest cry and our biggest fear. Love listens, always in every moment. Love hears.

"but God has surely listened and heard my prayer."

Psalm 66:19

Take a Moment to Listen

There is never a moment in time nor in eternity that I do not hear the cry of my beloved child. I am with you in your moments of doubt and pain, joy and uncertainty. I am with you lifting you higher, as I hold you close and bring peace to your frightened heart. Share with me all your thoughts, dreams, joys and sorrows for I would comfort your soul and guide your uncertain mind. Never doubt my presence, my child, as I am with you in absolute certainty at every moment. Trust in my love for you and know it is my joy to share in all your moments, for you are my child whom I love in time and through all of eternity.

Guided Meditation

Find your favorite spot to quiet your mind and rest. Take a deep breath and ask God to be with you. Have there been times where you felt God was with you and you were certain of his presence? What was that experience like? Did you ask God for something, or did you share what was on your mind? In thinking about that, were you more confident and comforted by your sharing and your prayer?

Think about how often you are aware of God's presence during the day. Take your time as you think about it. Do you often remember that God is with you, or do you get easily involved in your activities so that you forget his presence?

What do you imagine it would be like to remember God's presence more often? How would you feel knowing his presence was with you in all you were involved with? Is this something that you would like to experience? Can you sit with God now and let him know what is on your mind? Can you talk to him about helping you to be more aware of his presence and available guidance in your life? Sit quietly with God and try and listen to anything you think he wants you to know or understand. Take as long as you need, as he is always available. Then, let yourself feel his presence in peace and joy.

Your Thoughts/Experience

> "When we honestly ask ourselves which person in our lives means the most to us, we often find that it is those who instead of giving advice, solutions, or cures, have chosen rather to share our pain and touch our wounds with a warm and tender hand."
>
> Henri Nowen

Moving cautiously through the uncertainty of life, we are fortunate to find those that truly journey with us, listening with an open heart, sharing in our pain, fear and bewilderment. Offering no judgments, they look at us in neither disbelief, or disapproval. Instead, they remain close both in love and understanding. Here is one heart in need of healing, by another who is open to give. Here is compassion, empathy and a deep understanding. For as we feel understood, we feel whole once again. Love has touched our heart, and we are no longer alone. In those moments of shared emotional intimacy, our hearts begin to heal. As feeling understood touches our very deepest need.

Yet there is one who journeys with us unseen, holding our hearts in his delicate embrace. God listens and hears all the pain, fear and sorrow, all the while whispering love, encouragement and guidance, on each step of our uncertain road. We often do not acknowledge our unseen companion, yet love surrounds our hearts in every moment, healing us through our missteps, falls and self inflicted wounds. Love gently lifts us once again, as we continue to push forward, loving, and filling us with quiet peace. Here is the companion most needed, for here is love's healing touch.

> *"Be strong and courageous. Do not be afraid or terrified because of them, for the LORD your God goes with you; he will never leave you nor forsake you."*
>
> Deuteronomy 31:6

Take a Moment to Listen

Through all of your falls and missteps, I am here, lifting you up and whispering songs of eternal love. I journey with you as I take each moment in time and remind you of my eternal presence. My love will always heal your frightened heart, and fill you with the peace you have forgotten is your own. There is nothing to fear, for my love journeys with you, lifting you, guiding you and healing your soul. Turn to me just a little and I will take that moment filling your heart with healing peace. Let me be the companion that you seek, for I will always be the companion that comforts your heart.

Guided Meditation

As you sit in your most comfortable spot, take a deep breath. Take another and relax your whole body. Invite God to be with you. Take your time as you feel his presence within the deepest part of your heart.

Try to remember a moment when you felt God was truly with you. Try and remember what that felt like and what you experienced. What was it that made you so certain of God's presence? Was it a feeling, a sense or something that happened? What was it like to know you truly weren't alone?

Can you begin to use that experience of God's love and presence to remind yourself more often that God is with you? What do you think it would be like if you walked through life's journey more certain of his presence and his guidance? How do you think you would feel, and how would that affect the way you deal with decisions? What do you think you need to do to help you stay more focused on God's abiding presence? Think about what that might be. Take your time. Then ask God to help you. Listen to anything you think God wants you to know. Then sit with him quietly as you feel his presence and his healing peace.

Your Thoughts/Experience

> "We are already one. But we imagine that we are not. And what we have to recover is our original unity. What we have to be is what we are."
>
> Thomas Merton

Anaximander drew a map of the known world in the 6th century BC. Claudius Ptolomey drew the first map using lines of longitude and latitude in the 2nd century AD. While maps are important tools, especially if you need to get from point A to point B in any reasonable amount of time, they also make logical sense in understanding our known physical space giving us direction and a sense of location. Along with our sense of location, we accept identity in accordance with others who share that location including language, customs and beliefs. We proceed to build financial towers of importance, locking some into the system and locking others out. Smaller and smaller circles of people are 'normalized' while others are vilified. Maps are important tools, but they can be divisive.

Today's GPS systems are based upon maps that we accept as accurate. They take us from neighborhood to neighborhood, state to state, or country to country fairly safely. We can make temporary visits to areas that do not share our language, customs and beliefs. They can take us to 'foreign' territory. We are normalized. 'They' are foreign. From neighborhood to neighborhood, or country to country, we remain our own example for what is normal, real, safe and worthy while we deem, 'others' as not so much.

Neighborhood rivalries, boundary skirmishes, state conflicts and armed disagreements between nations are based upon what one group believes to be infringements upon another's 'norms'.

Further, understandings of ethics, morality and belief systems are justified by those locked into a system and justified by those locked out of that system. We are now not just divided, but splintered.

Lines of longitude and latitude and degrees of separation do not make us more or less human than any other. Neighborhoods, states and countries are places. They are locations. Our humanity extends across lines of demarcation. We are human beings with the same needs, with the same source. We have no lines and boundaries etched into our spirits.

> "Whatever exists has been named, and what humanity is has been known..."
>
> Ecclesiastes 6:10

Listen for a Moment

Holy child you are from the hand of holiness itself. All lay complete in heaven's arms, for there could be no lesser or greater in love's sight. How could love divide what is its very own? How could what was extended in completeness shun or deny its very being?

Guided Meditation

We usually see the world and our own community in a splintered way. There are those we identify with and the others that we do not. We can put up walls to keep ourselves enclosed within our own safe boundaries. Find a quiet spot where you can relax and feel God's peace. Invite God to be with you as you relax into his love.

Is there a group of people, or perhaps even a family or individual, whom you tend to stay away? Perhaps they have different customs, beliefs, or wear clothing that seems unfamiliar. Give yourself some time to really think about this. What do you think it is about this particular group that makes you feel this way? Have you had a difficult experience with someone from a similar group and assume that individual is the same? Are you unfamiliar with this group's customs and therefore decided you can't relate? What do you think is preventing you from opening up to someone who is different? As God to help you to understand what this might be about. How might your fear be getting in your way of reaching out?

Now sit with God in his peace and understanding and let him help you. Try and listen to whatever it is he might want you to understand. Listen. Then sit with God in his loving peace for as long as you need to—knowing you do not have to be afraid.

Your Thoughts/Experience:

> "We are shaped by our thoughts; we become what we think. When the mind is pure, joy follows like a shadow that never leaves."
>
> *Buddha*

Spend any time at all on a playground and in not so short a while amongst swings and climbing bars the sheer exuberance with which children feel their emotions is clear. Their defeats are grindingly sorrowful. Their delights are accompanied by hoots, howls and shrieks. Through scraped elbows, scuffed knees, moments of snacking, spinning, skipping and twirling children run the gamut of emotions heartfelt and pure. They tumble through their days without noticing the emotional flexibility through which they live moment to moment.

With the passing of time arrives the adult need to ruminate on each slight, sadness or rejection. Dissection of every social/emotional reaction held becomes a parlor game, as more and more time is spent on controlling and containing the spontaneous. When joy manages to unexpectedly break through it is met with shock, or caution, but rarely with the fullness once experienced as a child. Lost in the analysis of feeling, the feeling experience itself sits in the back of our life's repertoire and we are saddened and confused with what we perceive to be a grown-up life.

Adulthood needn't mean the ending of spontaneous joy, nor was it meant to be. Watch the young ones as they twirl through the springtime days of being. They have the answers we have forgotten in adulthood.

LOVE, GOD

> *"But I have calmed and quieted myself, I am like a weaned child with its mother; like weaned child I am content."*
>
> Psalm 131:2

Take a Moment to Listen

Precious child, there is no need to sacrifice the gift of joy for the perceived rewards of maturity. Within your unrestrained laughter is the song of life and hope, of growth and trust given freely by heaven itself. Safely, the gifts of joy graced to you through love's hand await your recognition as the reality of who you are and were created to be. Allow those gifts of joy and hope shine through your tired existence, for they indeed unlock your weary heart. It is through blessed joy that you are able to laugh, create, extend and grow. Allow yourself to be all of who in truth you are, for it is then that you become as free as the tenderness within which heaven holds you.

Guided Meditation

Sit in your comfortable space. Breathe in deeply and exhale completely. With each breath, you are embracing your own growth. Breathe in again deeply and exhale completely. With each breath inward allow yourself to feel the love and joy that surrounds you in every moment of life. Through all of the changes of life's experience you are gently cradled and held safely from all harm.

Choose to feel the gentleness of the love that fills you. Choose to feel this love in every moment.

Your Thoughts/Experience:

> *"Being deeply loved gives you strength; Loving deeply gives you courage."*
>
> *Lao Tzu*

Cycles are everywhere we look. There are cycles of seasons, cycles of harvest, cycles of life, physical cycles that are experienced and emotional cycles that we can watch unfold if we are vigilant enough to do so. The cycles to which we entrust our lives are perhaps the bedrock of all else.

To be sure, we are free to choose. We are the only ones who can freely choose. What might feel as a cycle chosen for us is, in reality, a choice we've made for ourselves. We can choose to entrust our life to a cycle of mistrust, caution and conservative care for others. We can also choose to entrust our life to a cycle of fear, withdrawal and resultant resentment. Whether we are aware of which cycle we have chosen to entrust our daily life, the fact remains that we, who have a choice, must choose and do choose which cycle of emotional energy we are trusting. Therein lies the rub so to speak.

Trusting in a divine love propels us forward with strength and courage to extend that love to all we meet. However, the human conundrum of wanting a written guarantee in triplicate before trusting in divine love is where we trip over our own fear while denying that the fear exists at all. Akin to overlapping juxtaposed cycles, we must choose again and again if we are to remain aware and honest in our participation. We are playing a shell game with ourselves if we do not.

Cycles are everywhere we look and are everywhere we cannot see. We are free to choose which cycle we frame our lives around. Choose wisely.

> "The wind blows to the south and turns to the north; round and round it goes. . ."
>
> *Ecclesiastes 1:6*

Take a Moment to Listen

Through all of the cycles of the early dawn to the twilight of night—I am here. Love encircles your heart through the cycles of days, seasons and the rhythm and hymn of creation. Choose my child to look at Love with an open heart and outstretched hand, for I would remind you always of all of the love and joy and peace that belongs to you. In each and every moment, choose my love and join with me in extending the love that is your birthright. In a season of fear, or a moment of trepidation look to me and remember that I will heal your heart and become your strength in an instant. For Love is within, as is all the peace your heart would hold.

Guided Meditation

Find your comfortable spot and sit. Sink into the space where you know is safe. Breathe in deeply and exhale completely. Breathe in again deeply and exhale completely. With each breath sink deeper into the space where you know is safe. Sink deeper into this space where you are embraced by divine love. Breathe in again, deeply and exhale completely.

Through all stages and trials of your lifetime, this space where you are loved completely grows as you grow. As you allow or choose love, Love answers bringing joy and peace to all you think and touch. Allow yourself to feel God's love in you and surrounding you. Stay in this space as long as you need.

Deborah J. Simmons-Roslak & Linda J. Orber

Your Thoughts/Experience:

Take a Moment to Listen

Beginnings are endings, just as endings are new beginnings, this then can be a new beginning if you will it be so. While there are always choices to be made, choosing to allow your self to be loved is the most important choice, and seemingly the most confusing. How is this so?

There is no fear or pain in Love. Neither greed nor compromise does it bring. Yet, in each moment of existence are you choosing that which can only bring you joy and peace? Are you choosing that which is your birthright by virtue of Love's hand?

There is no space love does not know, nor heart that love has forgotten. How could that be so? You were born from the song of heaven's Love for all the Beloved, crafted in tenderness, created to extend the love from whence you came.

As you live each day and in every moment allow the awareness of your hungry heart, then allow your heart nourishment. Listen to Love's song call to you, in however you can understand, for every heaven's child is sweetly cradled in the Heart that loved you first.

Bibliography

www.azquotes.com
www.biblehub.com NIV
www.brainyquotes.com
www.goodreads.com
www.pinterest.com
The Holy Bible –The New American Bible Copyright 1971

www.ingramcontent.com/pod-product-compliance
Lightning Source LLC
Chambersburg PA
CBHW050806160426
43192CB00010B/1665